"Equal parts funny, heartwarming, and inspiring—according to my careful calculations, this book is sure to be a hit!"
—Dr. Bunsen Honeydew, PhD, Esq

"A delightful and dazzling read no matter who *vous* are! Could have used more commentary about certain glamorous co-stars, though."
—Miss Piggy

"What one thing does this book have in common with a maze? You get lost in them! Wocka wocka!"
—Fozzie Bear

"Ate book. Tasty! Tasty!" —Animal

**KERMIT THE FROG** is an international film and television star, a humanitarian, an amphibitarian, and an educator. After his humble beginnings in the swamp, Kermit began his career on television in 1955. Since then Kermit has starred in numerous shows and films, including the Emmy Award–winning *The Muppet Show*, and has had a successful career as a recording artist, with hits like "Rainbow Connection." Kermit the Frog splits his time between the swamp and a pad in Hollywood, which he shares with pigs, bears, chickens, and various other weirdos.

# Before You Leap

## A Frog's-Eye View of Life's Greatest Lessons

First Edition, September 2006
First Hyperion Avenue Edition, April 2025
FAC-031939-24325
Printed in China

10 9 8 7 6 5 4 3 2 1

This book is set in Enzo OT
Designed by Stephanie Sumulong

Library of Congress Control Number: 2024936762
ISBN 978-1-368-10405-0
Reinforced binding

www.HyperionAvenueBooks.com

For the lovers, the dreamers, and you

# Thanks from the Frog

Y'know, when the publishing people came to me with the idea of rereleasing this book, I wasn't sure where to begin. Sure, the book was already written, but the world has changed a lot. I wondered what a frog like me had to say in the year 2025. So I did what I always do: I asked my friends for their advice. Miss Piggy reminded me that I had a contractual obligation to mention her in print at least three times annually. Gonzo reminded me that there are a lot of weirdos out there, and surely some of them still read books. But the best reminder probably came from Fozzie, who thought about it for a minute and then said, "Maybe there's someone out there who needs to hear your story." It was a good reminder that all of us Muppets have come a long way. And that one thing that keeps us going is this dream we have of making people happy. Maybe even inspiring those people to follow their own dreams. A lot has happened in the years since this book was first released, and I'll try to cover those things in the updates that follow. But, most importantly, I hope this book can serve as a bit of inspiration.

Before I launch into all my thank-yous to the folks who made this book possible, I want to begin by checking in on you. That's right—you. How are you doing? Did you drink enough water today? Are you sitting up straight? (Bad posture can really wreck a frog's back, let me tell you.) You're about to read all about how my friends and I got our start in show business and the lessons I've learned since then. And if there's anything you take away from this book, I hope it's this: There is room in the world for you and all your dreams, too.

As for the actual thank-you portion of this foreword, I'd like to thank my friends, The Muppets, for their encouragement along the way. Gosh, where to even begin? Miss Piggy, who is an inspiration in her own right. To Fozzie, for never-ending support. Thanks to Gonzo, even if his edits were not incorporated because the publishers could not, in fact, print this book on tapioca pudding. To my nephew, Robin, who is becoming quite the pint-size proofreader. I suppose I even owe a thank you to Statler and Waldorf, whose heckling is poignant even in writing.

I owe a special thank-you to my friend Jim Lewis, who spent his career helping Muppets like me find the right words. (Jim's retired now, but before he left, he was awarded the Gags Beasley Award for Excellence in Comedy—a real coveted award among joke writers.) I'd also like to thank my pals Leigh, Michael, Andy, Dani, Lisa, Alex, Ryan, and Frank at The Muppets Studio, and those strange guys Bill, Dave, David, Eric, Matt, and Peter who always seem to be standing around nearby.

There are a lot of other folks I want to thank, but there are only so many pages in a book. (And even if you're reading this digitally, those pixels aren't unlimited!) So I guess I'll sum it up by saying thank you to the people I've met along the way, and the people I've yet to meet. A friend of mine used to say, "It's a good life, enjoy it." All of those folks continue to make this a very good, very enjoyable life for a little frog from the swamp. So, uh—I guess I'll just say, Thank you.

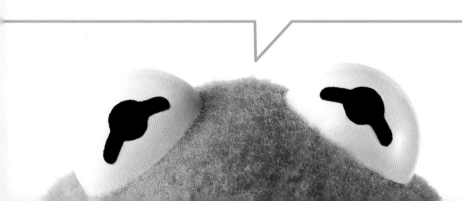

# CONTENTS

## Part 1: A Frog's Life

## Part 2: Lessons for Your Life

## Never Say Croak. . . . *—A very, very old frog proverb*

Hi-ho! Kermit the Frog here! As you probably guessed from the cover, the title, and all of these words, this is a book. Actually it's two books. First, it's a book about my life. Second, it's a book about your life. Let me explain.

The first part of the book—the part about my life—tells the story of how I got here, from growing up in the swamp to my long career in Hollywood and show business. (Please don't call it an autobiography; we frogs have a real problem with autos. Street-crossing is extremely stressful for your average amphibian.)

The second part to this book—the part about you—is even more important. Y'see, I didn't want to write just another

kiss-the-frog-and-tell celebrity memoir that Hollywood can turn into a low-budget special starring someone who looks nothing like me but tests really well with fourteen to thirty-nine-year-olds. I wanted to write a book that could actually make a difference in the life of the folks who read it; a book that can help you rise above the muck and mire and reach for rainbows, just like me.

I'm writing this because I want you to be inspired. I want to fill you with hope and encourage you to dream. I want you to leave your swamp, and set out on that most amazing and surprising journey: your life.

A good friend of mine, Jim Henson, captured this spirit perfectly when he said: "I believe that we form our own lives, that we create our own reality and that everything works out for the best. I know I drive some people crazy with what seems to be ridiculous optimism, but it has always worked for me."

Here's to being ridiculously optimistic.

Amphibiously yours,

*Kermit the Frog*

# PART 1
# A Frog's Life

I have to admit that I've had an extraordinary life so far. I've met kings, queens, presidents, and pigs. I've worked with some of the greatest talents of all time—actors, singers, dancers, athletes, and even a guy who can hang spoons from his nose. I've made movies, TV shows, music, and the occasional meme. And through it all, I've been surrounded by the best friends and finest fans a frog could ever want. This is my chance to tell that story.

It's also an opportunity to answer a lot of questions: How did a tadpole like me, born one of 2,353 brothers and sisters, make his way from the obscure and snake-infested swamps of his youth to the famous and, uh, snake-infested swamps of Hollywood? Who helped me, who influenced me, and what did I learn along the way?

This is also my chance to set the record straight. Let's face it, a lot has been said about my life over the years, most of it by Miss Piggy and her publicist. Here, at long last, I get my say.

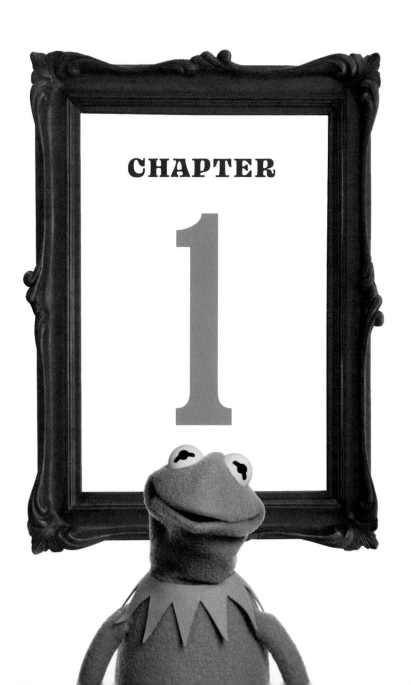

CHAPTER

1

# The Early Years

I have a lot of great memories from the swamp. I remember when I was little, we'd all just sit on our lily pads for hours and hours, rocking gently on the water and listening to the soft, sweet sound of chirping crickets. Then, of course, we'd eat the crickets . . . but that's another story.

## Back to the Swamp

The swamp will always be a part of me—and not just because you can never quite get that damp, sticky smell out once it soaks in. (Believe me, I've tried.) The swamp is who I am and where I come from; it's my birthplace and my hometown, my refuge and my strength, my past and my future. For me the swamp is where it all started, so let's start at the very beginning . . . back before I was born . . . back when the world was awash in primordial ooze . . . back at the dawn of time. (Okay, that's far enough.) Y'see, we frogs were drifting along with the continents and froggy-paddling through thick primeval muck in search of prehistoric mosquitoes small enough to eat.

At the risk of being called amphibi-centric, I really do believe that amphibians are the greatest group of species of all time. Think about it: We're equally at home on land and in the water, which automatically doubles our chances at the Summer Olympics; we have webbed feet—great for swimming, excellent for tap dancing; and, of course, having a long, sticky tongue to nab dinner means never waiting in long lines at trendy food trucks. Oh sure, I've said and sung about how hard it is being green, but I am—and I always have been—proud to be a frog.

Part of this pride comes from my family tree, which is a moss-covered willow, if you're curious. Generation after generation, members of my extended family have made their mark on history, including such notable relatives as:

**CLEOFROGTRA –** *who was the last web-footed ruler of Egypt, believed to be in de-Nile about her complicated relationship with snakes*

**EDGAR ALLEN TOAD** – *who was obsessed with croaking and wrote about it in his famous scary short story, A Tell-Tale Ribbet*

**AMELIA FROGHEART** – *who made history as the first amphibian to fly solo over the Atlantic Ocean—a real feat when you consider frogs dislike salt water*

**F. SCOTT FITZTADPOLE** – *who was renowned for his writings about life in the swamp during the roaring twenties and his particular fondness for daisies*

**ALBERT FROGSTEIN** – *who was the genius behind the amphibious equation defining tongue mass and bug catching-energy, Flea = MC$^2$*

**DR. FLYA ANGELOU** – *who is beloved in the frog community for her poems and memoirs, and had the same fondness for rainbows that I do*

## A Frog Is Born

I've always been fascinated by my family history. Knowing your past is important. And the more I learn about the people who came before me, the more inspired I am to carve my own place in this world of ours.

My own history begins more recently, in a little swamp just off the bayou halfway between hither and yon and just the other side of over there. (You can't miss it, unless you're trying to find it.) From the stories I've heard, my life's journey began on a hot, humid day in May. Above the hissing of snakes, chirping of birds, and kibitzing of alligators, there arose a shout of joy as my dad cried out for all the world to hear: "It's a boy and a girl and another boy and another girl and a boy and a boy and a boy and a boy and a boy and a girl and a girl and a girl and a girl and a girl and twelve more boys and fourteen more girls," and so forth and so on . . . ad amphibeum.

When Dad had recovered his voice and Mom had gotten over her ad nauseam, our happy little family numbered 2,353 tadpoles. (As with all frog families, the number of siblings is always approximate. We tadpoles tend to mix and mingle upon entering the swamp, making an accurate head-and-tail count almost impossible, except for tax purposes.)

Checking out old photos of Mom & Dad.

## My Parents: Mom and Dad Frog

Gee, I loved them. Still do. They were good to me. They were good to all of us. From the very first day we were born, they urged every one of us to follow our dreams— or at least to go someplace else to play so they could finish their dinner in peace. Somehow, despite the sheer volume of lunches they had to pack, playdates they had to organize, and nightly bedtime rituals they had to remember and repeat, they found time to spend with each of us. We weren't just another mouth to feed or another tail to diaper; we were each treated like individuals. Okay, so they did make us all wear "Hello My Name Is . . ." tags until we were almost in our teens.

Hey, it's not easy to remember 2,353 names, especially when every single one of your kids is green and goggle-eyed.

## Good Ol' Dad

What can I tell you about my dad? Over the years, folks have asked me so many questions about him: What's he like? Do you two get along? And, of course, was your dad in show business? Would he be interested in appearing as a contestant on a new streaming series about celebrity parents?

I'll answer the second to last question first: No. Dad never appeared onstage. In fact, I can't remember him ever appearing on dry land of any kind. But he was a natural comic, with a gift for dancing the soft-shoe. (This despite the fact that he never wore shoes.) No matter what I do in my life, Dad will always be my first and greatest role model. It would be presumptuous for me to say we're a lot alike. Oh sure, we're both short and green with spindly arms and legs and a voice that gets high-pitched and squeaky whenever we get excited or mad or tired or . . . Okay, so Dad and I are a lot alike. But there's more to him than just being spindly, squeaky, and green. Y'see, my dad is an old-fashioned dad. Oh, he doesn't smoke a pipe, wear a cardigan, or take us into his den for frog-to-tadpole talks. In the swamp, pipes get wet, cardigans get moldy, and dens are usually filled with bears. My dad was—and still is—my hero: always there to give advice, to lend a helping hand, and to encourage us to be the best we can be.

Over the years, I've tried my darnedest to live up to Dad's example, giving advice and encouragement to those I've met along the way. When folks say they admire my ability to deal with all the craziness and chaos that come from working with The Muppets, they are really complimenting my father and the lessons he taught me. Thanks, Dad.

## "WOW" Spelled Upside Down

Naturally, when it comes to family, Dad couldn't have done it without Mom. "Mom." I just like saying that word. Did you ever notice that "Mom" is "wow" spelled upside down? (I did, but then again, I spend a lot of hours sitting on logs waiting for fireflies to tire out so I can grab a light snack.) If there was ever a mother who put the "wow" in Mom, it's mine. I'm sure you feel the same way about your own mother. No matter how great a dad is, there's something even more special about a mom—a heartfelt bond that's difficult to explain and impossible to break.

My mom gave all of us lots of affection and understanding, but she could also be a tough taskmaster. For instance, she would always make sure that I brushed my teeth after every meal. Now, that may not sound like a big deal, except for the fact that—as you may have noticed—I don't have any teeth! That didn't matter to Mom; personal hygiene is personal hygiene, and no child of hers is going out in the world without a thorough brushing and flossing. Mom could also

> I guess my show-business bug comes from Mom. No, it wasn't another meal she made; it was her second career.

be very demanding when it came to table manners: "Take your turn, and no reaching!" This is good advice, especially when you're a frog who eats with your tongue. Whenever my sisters, brothers, and I broke Mom's rule, dinner ended as a tongue-tied mess that took hours to untangle.

I guess my show-business bug comes from Mom. No, it wasn't another meal she made; it was her second career. You see, in addition to feeding and rearing our oversize family, Mom also had a very successful business career as talent booker for the local swamp theater, the Bayou Bijou. Working out of her playbill- and flypaper-littered office, Mom would audition and book top local talent to perform at the theater. Long before you could text message your vote for the next great singing idol, there was Mom, finding hidden talent in the swamp. Some of her discoveries included future showbiz greats like Lilly Ponds, the Lipizzaner Horseflies, and Moe Green and His Vegas Cuties.

But Mom's biggest job, and the one she did best of all, was taking care of us. (She hugged us when we got scared, kissed us when we needed love, and chased away our blues with a smile—or, if they were especially pesky, with a flyswatter.) To this day, just hearing the sound of my mom's voice fills me with a feeling of happiness and warmth that even her Fly-Shoe Pie can't match. To me, she was, is, and always will be the world's best mom. Wow, indeed!

# Mom's Famous Fly-Shoe Pie

## INGREDIENTS

1 heaping tablespoon of Algae
1 pinch of Fungus
4 cups of Pond Water
3/4 cup of Sunflower Seeds

1 dollop of Honey
1 Shoe
3 cups of fresh Flies

## DIRECTIONS

1. Grate the Algae and pinch the Fungus. If the Algae is grating on you, pinch it, too.
2. Carefully separate the Pond Water from the pond scum. Save the pond scum for later. It makes a delicious dessert topping.
3. While nibbling on the Sunflower Seeds—which have nothing to do with this recipe but sure are mighty tasty, yesiree—use your dolloper to dollop Honey all over the Shoe. A loafer is perfect for casual meals, but a high heel or wingtip works best for formal dinners. If you're planning to eat and run, use a sneaker.
4. Sprinkle 3 cups of fresh Flies over the now sticky Shoe and enjoy!

# SWAMPED! Raising a Family of 2,353

Mom and Dad sure had their hands full with us kids. If you're a parent, you know how hard it can be to keep just a couple of offspring happy, healthy, and not screaming at each other morning, noon, and night. Now imagine that typical family dynamic times 2,353—not counting visiting cousins, the neighborhood toads, and the occasional salamander who dropped by to share a meal. We were a boisterous brood who would have raised the roof off the house if only we'd had a roof . . . or a house.

If you think that raising children is a challenge, try tadpoles. The pitter-patter of lots of little feet is nothing compared to the swish-swash of a thousand tiny tadpole tails. And if there's one thing that tadpoles love to do, it's skitter around the swamp. Of course, when your legs haven't grown in yet, skittering is pretty much all you can do.

Now, if you're a parent you already know that it's virtually impossible to bathe, bottle, and burp babies when they're squirming—or skittering. So what did my mom and dad do? Simple! They did what all other overwhelmed parents do in that situation: They called in the grandparents. Sure enough, as soon as Grandma and Grandpa the Frog showed up at our tide pool, we kids would all come skittering over so they could spoil us with songs, stories, and candied caterpillars. And while we were distracted, Mom and Dad would scoop us up (literally) in groups of a hundred or so and get us ready for bed. I'm not recommending this method to all parents. Apparently some kids aren't big on candied caterpillars; go figure! But it sure worked for us.

As I look back on those tadpole years, I realize just how fun and carefree they were. But to be honest, back then I didn't think it was all that great being a tadpole. My sisters, brothers, and I just wanted to grow up—and grow up just as fast as we could!

See, when you're small, all you ever think about is getting big. (Even if you're like me, and "big" means about twenty-four inches tall.) Kids can't wait to stretch their legs, leave their tail behind, and get on with life. You probably felt the same way when you were young—except maybe for the part about the tail. But then, as the years go by, you begin to understand just how precious those tadpole days are and how quickly they pass.

I believe that sentimentality is important. It helps us appreciate all the wonderful moments of our life. I know I try to appreciate them every single day, even when I'm out there making new memories.

# Lessons from the Swamp

I used to think that the swamp was simply where I was raised. Now I realize what a great environment it was—in every sense of the word.

Everyone knows that a swamp is an amazing ecosystem overflowing with all the flora and fauna you can shake a stick at—if that's your idea of a good time. But few realize that a swamp is the world's most diverse interspecies community. It has toads, salamanders, snakes, lizards, alligators, birds, bees, and all the insects you can eat. Look at any wetland area and you'll discover as varied and unusual a cross section of humanity (and nonhumanity) as you'll find anywhere this side of a downtown bus terminal.

Our swamp was like a semi-submerged Ellis Island, a place where you could always find your tired, your poor, your huddled muskrats yearning to breathe free, plus plenty of teeming shores overflowing with wretched refuse. (Attention, campers: Reconsider before you litter!)

When you're constantly surrounded by such a varied group, you learn to respect other points of view. You learn to live in harmony and appreciate differences. That's an important life skill for everyone, especially those of us who work with pigs, bears, rats, and various weirdos. (I know I'm not the only one.)

## Frog School: It's Not Easy Getting A's

Although we tadpoles learned a lot just living in the swamp, that doesn't mean we didn't have to go to school. In fact, some of the happiest years of my youth were spent learning the ropes, vines, and other hanging vegetation at my alma mater, good old P.S. 1170 (home of the Phighting Amphibians).

You may wonder what a frog can learn in school. After all, isn't most frog behavior instinctive? Ah, if only it were that easy being green! The truth is, amphibians have to study hard to master the finer points of frogosity.

All in all, my Frog School years were swell. I look back on class pictures—with me and my best buddies, like Croaker the Frog—and wonder where the years went.

But the toughest part of growing up still lay ahead—or, to be more accurate, atail—of me. My tadpole days were numbered. The time was coming when I would no longer be a skittering tadpole, when I would finally become a full-fledged frog without that tail dragging behind me!

## The Day I Got My Legs!

Most humans set off on their own later in life. But for a tadpole becoming a frog, this life-changing event occurs in the amphibian equivalent of the awkward teen years. Our voices change and our eyes usually get smaller—although in my case they stayed oddly large and ping-pongy (a look that would serve me well when I went into television, but more on that later). Most important of all, we grow legs.

Growing legs is a major event for a frog—and for the entire world of French cuisine. Frogs' legs make it possible for us to set foot on dry land or a mildly muddy patch of muck. After all, if it weren't for legs, we frogs would be fish. Not that there's anything wrong with that; some of my best friends are trout.

When the big day came, I remember standing there knee-deep in the swamp with my parents—and a couple hundred of my brothers and sisters who happened to also be ready to hop that day—knowing that my life would never again be the same. At last, I was footloose and fancy-free, ready to pursue my dream and start my search for that elusive Rainbow Connection. (CUE MUSIC: If this were a movie, there'd be a song here.)

*My fresh new legs! Can't you tell?*

CHAPTER

2

# Discovering the Magic Store

**A** lot of entertainers find the same joy they felt in childhood when they perform, and there's a special magic that comes from finding others who share that joy. It's exactly how I felt when I found The Muppets and started performing. We call it the Magic Store—the feeling of belonging that comes from singing, dancing, and making people happy.

## Getting Started in Showbiz

If you've seen *The Muppet Movie*, you may remember the opening scene, where I'm sitting on a log playing the banjo and singing "Rainbow Connection." Moments later a lost Hollywood agent drifts in, "discovers" me, and suggests that I head off to Hollywood, where auditions are being held for frogs who want to become rich and famous.

Over the years, I've been asked about this scene many times: Was I actually discovered in the swamp? Are Hollywood agents ever lost? Well, the truth is that there's a bit of fact and fiction mixed in. For instance, Hollywood agents are lost all the time; in fact, I've never met one who wasn't lost—usually while carrying someone else's residual check. But as for being discovered in the swamp—well, that's where Hollywood stretched the truth just a little. I actually had to go out to the dirt road just beyond the fallen oak tree to get discovered. (Sure, it's a small change, but I'm trying to be accurate here.)

And once I was discovered, I knew it was time for this young and still-wet-behind-the-ears (what ears?) frog to start chasing his dream.

I remember that sunny summer morning when I left the swamp. My mom, my dad, and all my brothers and sisters gathered at that dirt road at the edge of the swamp to say good-bye. This did not make for a quick getaway; when you have a big family like mine, saying good-bye usually takes about three days. But when the farewells were over, I hopped on my bicycle and pedaled down that long, dusty road with my banjo on my knee. I didn't know which way I was going or where this road would take me, but quickly learned an important lesson that has stayed with me to this day: Never pedal a bicycle with a banjo on your knee. It's unsafe, and very painful.

Although I may not have had a clue about where I was headed, I did know a thing or two about what I was willing to do to make it in show business.

I'd take any job. Whether it was painting scenery or being greenery, a gig was a gig. I'd do all my own stunts. A good thing, too. Even today, short green stuntmen are few and far between. I'd be a best boy or a production assistant or work craft services. Looking back now, all of my early work gave me a deeper understanding of how the entertainment industry functions, and also gave me a deep appreciation for everyone's job on set. It truly is a team effort!

## A Fellow Dreamer

Around this time, I met someone who had a big impact on my career. His name: Jim Henson. I'm not exactly sure what he did, but whatever it was really moved me. Jim and I met in Washington, DC, where he'd been given a small broadcast segment on local television, back when local television was black-and-white and only had a few channels. Jim was always busy around the set—writing a script, making a prop, or just giving me a lift. But Jim was so much more than a handy man; he had an incredible sense of fun and a remarkable spirit that made you believe absolutely anything was possible. And he wasn't afraid to roll up his

A fellow dreamer, Jim Henson.

sleeves and make it happen.

Jim and I had a relationship that just kept growing over the years. It was as if we were part of each other, connected at the heart. Like me, Jim believed anything was possible if you dreamed big and worked hard enough. I truly believe that because of Jim and his dreams, the world really is a better place—not just for me, but for all of us.

With Jim's helping hand, I was ready to reach higher than I'd ever imagined. The time had come to take a bite out of the Big Apple.

## Kermit Takes Manhattan

Long before The Muppets took Manhattan, New York City took me in with open arms. I loved the city: The subway smelled like a swamp; taxicabs made crossing the streets impossible for everyone, not just frogs; and even the Statue of Liberty was green!

When I first arrived in New York, I naturally wanted to make it on Broadway. But except for a few nonspeaking walk-on parts in the play *The Night of the Iguana*, roles for frogs were hard to come by.

Lucky for me, there was a lot of other work in New York—for me and for the peculiar troupe of players that was by then officially known as The Muppets. Like all young actors struggling to make it in the city, we Muppets shared everything. We ate together, lived together, went to parties together, and even auditioned for the same shows.

And we'd work almost anywhere to make ends meet. I even worked as a waiter for a while at Jambes de la Grenouille, an exclusive French restaurant on the Upper East Side. Then one day I found out what Jambes de la Grenouille meant and discovered my picture in the menu under "specials du jour." I hopped the next cab out of there and never went back.

All in all The Muppets in those days were a rowdy and rambunctious group. (We haven't changed much.) We were always under each other's feet (at least those of us who have feet), and frankly I don't know how we all lived together in such a small space. And I'm talkin' really small.

**How small was it? It was so small that when I brought in the welcome mat, we had wall-to-wall carpeting. ***

But we didn't care because we were all working in showbiz and loving it! By that time, The Muppets had made regular appearances on many of the biggest variety shows of the day. Well, maybe not "regular" appearances. Let's face it: When it comes to Muppets, there's nothing regular about our appearance.

All of this exposure led to lots of wonderful things. We did dozens of television commercials for everything from Chinese food to soap to toothpaste. Advertisers liked the way that viewers were strangely attracted to our strangeness, though still to this day no one can quite explain it.

While the rest of us were struggling, Rowlf the Dog had landed a regular spot on TV . . . and in the occasional dog food commercial. As the first of The Muppets to become famous, Rowlf taught all of us important lessons about not letting fame go to your head. (These were lessons that Miss Piggy obviously skipped.)

* *Joke courtesy of Fozzie Bear.*

Among the important things Rowlf taught me about being famous are:

**YOU SHOULD NEVER BITE THE HAND THAT FEEDS YOU.** It's not kind. It's not sanitary. And rabies shots hurt like the dickens.

**IT'S NICE TO BE IMPORTANT, BUT IT'S IMPORTANT TO BE NICE.** If you treat people like a dog, they'll treat you the same, which isn't half bad if you're a dog, but otherwise isn't much fun.

**YOU CAN'T TAKE IT WITH YOU.** Which is why Rowlf was so generous with sharing his salary, though he was known to bury bonuses in the backyard.

**IT'S BETTER TO GIVE THAN TO RECEIVE.** (See rabies shots reference, above.)

Rowlf not only showed us how to handle fame, he made sure we all shared in his success. When Rowlf went out to a fancy dinner, he always came back with a doggy bag for all of us. If he rode in a limo, we all rode in the limo. If he chased a limo, we all chased the limo. If he caught the limo, we all buried the limo.

From those early days through his pun-riddled years as Dr. Bob of Veterinarian's Hospital on *The Muppet Show* and right up to today, Rowlf remains the best doggone friend a frog could ever have.

Rowlf's success meant that more and more folks were interested in The Muppets. Before you knew it, we were all making appearances and all kinds of specials. I even booked a gig as a roving reporter on a new television program for kids! But the one I was most excited about? *The Frog Prince*. For the first time ever, I would be billed on-screen as a frog. Times were changing. Finally I could come out and tell the world that I, Kermit, was an amphibian and proud of it! No more webfoot backlash or unwarranted wart jokes! No more pretending I was a chameleon, ready to change just to blend in! To borrow the phrase, I was finally finding my home at the Magic Store.

CHAPTER

3

# Finding the Rainbow Connection

*T*he Muppets were becoming a household name. But more in a "limited TV appearance" sort of way. Certainly not in a "headlining their own show" way. At least not yet. But all of that was about to change. . . .

## At the Corner of Hollywood & Swine

Can you picture this? A frog knocks on your door. You let him in. Before you know it, he's taken out a glossy full-color brochure and a really nifty felt-board presentation and launched into his lively over-the-top spiel for a new kind of half-hour, prime-time, big-budget television show featuring celebrity guest stars and a still-unknown cast of Muppets and other creatures. And we'll call it (drum roll, please):

Picture that same frog out on the sidewalk dusting off his collar, scratching his head, wondering what the heck just happened and whether he'll ever get back his glossy full-color brochure and really nifty felt-board presentation. Now you have a pretty good idea what it was like trying to convince the world that it needed a frog-hosted variety television show.

THUNK! THUMP! Oh good, they just tossed the brochure and the felt board back out on the sidewalk. Time to go to the next network.

For some reason no one wanted to buy our show, at least not at first. We heard all kinds of reasons why a show like this would "never work"; here are some of my favorites:

> *"You should have come in last week. We've already got a frog-hosted weekly variety television show in development."*
>
> *"We absolutely love the concept, except for the part about it being a prime-time, big-budget show featuring celebrity guest stars and a still-unknown cast of Muppets and other creatures."*
>
> *"Why a frog?"*
>
> *"I love The Muppets. You guys I never cared for, but I adore The Muppets."*
>
> ## "SECURITY!!!!!"

But we didn't give up. We were determined to go to every network to pitch our idea, which didn't take too long because there were only three networks back then. Eventually, a kind network executive decided to give us a chance (either that or he got tired of stepping over us when we refused to budge from his doorway). In any case, we got our break. They were going to let us make a television special that would serve as what's called a "backdoor pilot." (That means if they don't like it, they throw you out the back door.) And to show we were willing to "play ball" with the network, we gave this special a name that would appeal to the refined sensibilities of our high-class adult viewing audience. The title: *The Muppet Show: Sex and Violence.*

It was a funny show, but I didn't get to be the host. That role was taken by a very nice, professional variety show host named Nigel, who tested better with focus groups, key demographics, and members of his immediate family, except for his in-laws, who didn't much care for him. We did well in the overnights, but the next morning, there we were out the back door, dusting off our collars, scratching our heads, and wondering what the heck just happened.

# Crossing the Pond to Stardom

Having run out of television networks in America, there was only one thing to do: leave the country. So we loaded up our brochures, felt boards, and entire cast in a couple of wooden crates and had ourselves shipped to England. Now there's something about the English, who see absolutely nothing odd about letting a frog and a bunch of crazies have their own variety show. I don't know if there is a long-standing British tradition or whether the whole country just went daft for a wee bit, but whatever the reason, Lord Lew Grade invited us over to England. He was a real showman. He loved to do what The Muppets loved to do—put on a show and entertain the world! It was through his wisdom, generosity, and willingness to take a chance on something outlandish and silly that, at long last, *The Muppet Show* was born.

Now, the only thing in show business that's more difficult than coming up with an idea for a show and selling that idea is when you actually have to put on the show! All of sudden, after years of waiting and wanting, we had to deliver the goods: an entire season's worth of top-notch, high-quality, professional show-business entertainment. (Or at least the Muppet equivalent thereof.) Naturally, when faced with such a daunting task, we did what The Muppets always do in situations like this: PANIC!!!!

## The Show Must Go On . . . Somehow

After much running around, shrieking in high-pitched voices, and waving our arms in the air, we realized panicking alone was not going to get the job done. Oh sure, it might be entertaining enough to fill one half-hour show, but what about the rest of the series? So we put our panic aside—temporarily—and got down to business.

The first thing we needed was a place to do the show. We considered putting on

Statler

the show from those cargo boxes in which we'd been shipped to England, but we quickly decided it was better to think outside the box. As luck would have it, space became available at a local theater that oddly enough went by the name of The Muppet Theatre. Owned by the great real estate tycoon J. P. Grosse and managed by his overeager nephew, Scooter (soon to be our stage manager), this theater had everything we were looking for: atmosphere, panache, and a stage. It even came with its own stagehands! Okay, so they were rats; we realized it was cheaper to hire them than to fumigate.

As an added attraction (distraction? disruption? all of the above?), the theater even had its own built-in, state-of-the-art hecklers. Statler and Waldorf, those two old gentlemen in the balcony, would soon become a fixture in our theater and in our lives. Why did they come to all of our performances even though they obviously disliked and disparaged everything we did? I'd try to explain it, but I haven't a clue. And besides, I understand that Statler and Waldorf are still working on their very own memoir—*Today Is the First Day of What's Left of Your Life*. (Their book has been in development with Curmudgeonly Press for over two decades, so surely something should be published soon.)

With rats, hecklers, and a nepotism-induced stage manager already on the payroll, it was time to throw open the stage doors and hope that our cast would show up. And boy, did they ever!

In show business, when you hold open auditions, it's

Waldorf

39

called a "cattle call." At our audition, that's exactly who turned up: cattle, as well as bears, pigs, penguins, fish, chicken, monsters, and creatures of every size, species, and entertainment orientation. At first I was surprised and overwhelmed, but after recovering for a few days at a nearby bed-and-breakfast, I realized that this kind of talent could make our show unique, or maybe notorious, in the world of show business. Y'see, as an equal-opportunity show, we welcomed everyone, no matter how strange or obscure their talents. And that's always been The Muppets' Way. We don't care who you are, what you look like, or what you can do. If you want to be part of our show, then you're part of our show, as long as you can find a place to stand, lie down, or wedge yourself into a corner.

> **And that's always been The Muppets' Way. We don't care who you are, what you look like, or what you can do.**

Among those who found a place on our stage were dozens of performers who would later become household names—even if only in the households where they happened to be living at the time. Stars like my sweet-voiced nephew Robin the Frog, Marvin Suggs and and His Muppaphone, Sweetums, Lew Zealand and His Boomerang Fish, Pops, Hilda from wardrobe, Crazy Harry, the Flying Zucchini Brothers, Link Hogthrob, Beauregard, Wayne and Wanda, the Newsman, Benson and his Baby Band . . . to name just a few. These performers and many more like them were sure to make our show outrageous, unpredictable, dangerous, and mesmerizingly weird.

## Expanding our Cast

But we were still missing those one-of-a-kind specialists who would appeal to underserved members of the audience.

For instance, for those interested in science, or at least nifty experiments gone awry, we established Muppet Labs ("Where the Future Is Being Made Today"), staffed by two of the finest minds available at the time—Dr. Bunsen Honeydew and his faithful assistant, Beaker. Immediately, we were at the forefront of the scientific television variety show field, far ahead of anyone else (in the highly unlikely event that anyone else was foolish enough to follow us into this field).

As for space exploration, it was widely believed at the same time that the "final frontier" had finally been reached. But we knew there were new worlds to explore, so we launched "Pigs in Space," to follow the inane adventures of the SS Swinetrek as we drifted aimlessly through the cosmos. With this segment, we immediately grabbed the attention of outer space aficionados desperate for anything to watch.

Another key area of interest was food. Although everyone eats it, we learned that few, if any, shows offered the food's point of view. We remedied that situation by featuring the inexplicable culinary endeavors of the legendary Swedish Chef. Here was someone who could get food to disagree with you even before you ate it.

Oh, and if you're wondering, we're not entirely sure he's really Swedish. No one I've ever met from Sweden is familiar with the term "Børk børk børk." Come to think of it, no one I've ever met from the culinary world thinks he's a chef. Nevertheless, the segment was entertaining for everyone except the ingredients and the diners.

So what better way to follow up a meal like that than with a trip to the hospital? In our case, "Veterinarian's Hospital," the continuing story of a quack who has gone to the dogs. With my old pal Rowlf the Dog doing a turn as that surgical cut-up Dr. Bob, along with his equally punishing nurse staff, this feature on our show gave the medical profession a taste of its own medicine.

Finally, we knew there would be viewers out there who thought that everything we did was annoying, disturbing, and patriotically suspect. So rather than ignore these malcontents, we gave them their own on-the-air malcontent, the ever-irking, never-shirking Sam Eagle.

Still something was missing. If we were going to do a musical variety show, we'd need music! Oh sure, we had Nicky Napoleon and His Emperor Penguins, with the always-available Nigel serving as maestro. But we also needed a hip, happening music group, one that would attract the demographically desirable hip, happening audience that was too lazy to get up to change the channel. There was only one music group that fit this bill; unfortunately, The Beatles had disbanded a few years earlier. So we turned to those other, uh, giants of rock and roll, Dr. Teeth and the Electric Mayhem. It had the melodious merchant of music Dr. Teeth at the keyboard, the totally awesome Janice on lead guitar, the habitually groovy Floyd Pepper on bass, the mumbling and mellow Lips on

Dr. Teeth and the Electric Mayhem

trumpet, and the laconic yet strangely lucid Zoot on sax. This group was hip, happening, loud, and most important of all, available. Plus it had this drummer named Animal.

People often ask me what Animal is really like, so let me tell you briefly. He's an appetite with legs, a force of nature who is wild about percussion. But there's another side to Animal; he's an angel with a heart of gold, a love of bunny rabbits, and a generous spirit, and he will help anyone who doesn't stand between him and his pursuits. We're lucky to have him—and we're lucky he's usually chained.

At last it was time to play the music, time to light the lights, time to put on makeup, time to dress up right, time to raise the curtain on—

Not quite yet. I sensed something was *still* missing. It was a splash of derring-do, a slap of what-was-that, and a hearty haymaker of you-won't see-this-anywhere-else-thank-goodness. At the very moment I was mulling over these musings (or is it musing over these mullings?), in the door— or rather through the ceiling—came the Great Gonzo! If I knew then what I know now, I still wouldn't be able to make sense of what Gonzo does or what Gonzo is. All I know is that he's the only one we could find to hum "The Flight of the Bumblebee" while devouring a steel-belted radial tire. That's unique! That's bizarre! That's good enough for me. In addition to being an unfathomable talent, he's a great friend and the very best chicken-dating, daredevil performance artist I've ever seen—and I've seen them all.

## Time to Open the Curtain

Now, without a doubt, *The Muppet Show* was ready to go on the air!

And it was! And we did! And I know what you're thinking: Isn't there someone I forgot to mention? Miss Piggy. On our very first show, she was part of The Muppet Show Glee Club. The very definition of a breakout star. From the git-go, this pig was gittin' and goin'. No sooner did The Muppet Show Glee Club begin to sing the song "Temptation" on that very first *Muppet Show* than Miss Piggy pushed her way front and center, throwing herself into the spotlight. (Truth be told, Miss Piggy had a small part in a sketch called "Return to Beneath the Planet of the Pigs" in our original pilot, but it was clear that she'd made up her mind to never play a small part again.) She simply insisted she be front and center, and since then has become a permanent, irremovable part of our show, your world, and my life.

Let me say that I have nothing but fondness for Miss Piggy. I respect her courage, her character, her chutzpah, her joie de vivre, and even her faux French. Few have done so much for so long to make sure they were noticed by so many. And nobody does what Miss Piggy does as frequently or relentlessly as she does it, whatever it is. Yes, Miss Piggy is one of a kind . . . for which I am eternally grateful.

That said, there are certain misconceptions, falsehoods, and outright fibs about her and me. It seems that no matter what I do or where I go, everyone wants to know the "truth" about my relationship with her. My answer is: We are very close friends who work together, and who knows what the future holds.

Let's face it: Piggy and I have had more ups and downs, on-again-off-agains, was-the-wedding-real-or-not twists and turns than there are hyphens in this sentence. We've played scenes together where we're married, we've shared a TV show plot where we broke up, and we've made waves in the press with changes in our relationship status. If you were hoping this edition of the book would include all new kiss-and-tell details, I'm sorry to disappoint you. I'm just a frog who likes his privacy.

I will say this: I have the greatest respect and affection for her. And I'm glad she pushed her way to the front of the chorus all those years ago. She's one of the great celebrities of this or any generation. Like it or not, without Miss Piggy, The Muppets wouldn't be where we are today . . . and neither would I.

## And Now Finally . . . It's The Muppet Show

With our very special guest (YOUR NAME HERE). YAAAAAY!!!

From the very first, we didn't know what we were getting into, and neither did the guest stars or the audience. Yet for reasons that remain a mystery to this day, the show struck a chord with people around the world. This is either a credit to our work or proof positive that the world is filled with a lot of very strange people with struck chords. Whatever the case, we were on the air and across the globe, seen in more than a hundred countries by as many as 235 million people each week.

For five seasons and 120 shows, the audience embraced us—the world's first interspecies television variety show.

## A Little Something for Everyone

We did our best to appeal to the broadest possible audience. Let's face it—singing vegetables, talking rocks, tap-dancing frogs, and marauding Viking pigs were the kinds of entertainment you just couldn't find anywhere else at the time. (Of course, this was before reality TV and daytime talk shows made these sorts of things commonplace.) As promised in our original sales pitch for the show, we had something for everyone: "Small children will love the cuddly, cute characters. Young people will love the fresh, innovative comedy. College kids and intellectual eggheads will love the underlying symbolism of everything. And freaky, long-haired, dirty, cynical hippies will love our freaky, long-haired, dirty, cynical Muppets." And sure enough, they did!

But for all the backstage insanity and onstage inanity we threw into the show, I believe that one thing above all others made *The Muppet Show* such an international phenomenon. And that, of course, was our very special guest stars. All 120 of them!

Interviewers and fans always ask me, "Who was your favorite guest star?" I can honestly say they all brought something unique and special to the show. And that was what made *The Muppet Show* so great—the variety of guests from the worlds of classic theater, dance, cinema, TV, comedy, music, and pop culture. We were so fortunate that they would come to our show week after week and share their talents, but also share their sense of play. Classic actors would sing. Comedians would dance. Musicians would act. *The Muppet Show* became a place where you could be a little weird and a little silly because you were surrounded by a group of Muppets who were a little weird and a little silly. I'm so grateful to each of our very special guests for sharing the Magic Store with us.

# Hooray for Hollywood!

In the midst of all this, Hollywood beckoned. Okay, so they didn't exactly beckon, but they did forget to lock the front gate at the studio, and for The Muppets that was as good as an open invitation to make a movie.

Casting our first movie wasn't all that difficult. We figured that it would be best if we were in it.

As for the story, well, as I said earlier, it was loosely based on our true story. Okay, very loosely. Okay, so we made most of it up. But gee, isn't that what Hollywood is all about?

Our biggest problem was coming up with a name for that first movie. Many suggestions were market tested, focus grouped, bandied about, and throttled

to within an inch of their life by committees.

Finally, after realizing that the audience deserved to know what they were getting into, we decided to be up front about the whole thing and call it *The Muppet Movie*. We opened to great reviews, and the audience showed up in droves—though some took mass transit because droves were hard to drive. (And when they came out of the movie, what did each and every one of them want to know? "How did you ride that bicycle?")

Sheesh! You'd think folks had never seen a frog ride a

bicycle before. I mean, think of all the famous frog-riding-a-bicycle movies over the years. Such classic cinematic achievements as . . . well, there was . . . and who can forget . . . Okay, so it was something of a first. But we frogs have been riding bikes for years, and it's true: Once you learn, you never forget.

The success of our first movie led to a second movie, which we were going to call *The Muppet Movie II*, but with all of the sequels being released, roman numerals were in short supply, so we instead choose *The Great Muppet Caper*. I had always wanted to do a caper movie, and the gang always wanted to see if we could put "Great" and "Muppet" in a title without being sued for false advertising. Shockingly enough, not only weren't we sued, we had another box-office success. And before anyone could stop it, we made yet another movie—*The Muppets Take Manhattan*. This film was the easiest to name because The Muppets were in the movie and it took place in Manhattan. At early screenings the movie was known as *The Muppets Doing a Movie Taking Place in Manhattan*, but it was quickly shortened after complaints filed by the Movie Marquee Sign Hangers Union.

After the success of *The Muppet Show* and these three movies, we were a force to be reckoned with in Hollywood. Well, actually, Miss Piggy was the force to be reckoned with; the rest of us just kind of followed in her wake, bobbing along atop the waves she inevitably made. At this point—according to press materials released by Piggy's high-powered PR firm—we began working with some of the biggest names in the business. Famous writers like Charles Dickens and Robert Louis Stevenson begged us to make their books into movies.*

Making movies like *The Muppet Christmas Carol* and *Muppet Treasure Island* was a big departure for us. For the first time, we had to portray characters other than ourselves. For me that meant going back to acting school to prepare for my roles in these movies. I took classes in the Stanislavski Method, Meisner Training, the Alexander Technique, Brechtian Acting, and Method Acting before finally settling on that time-honored Muppet method of Over Acting.

I also did extensive research. To play Bob Cratchit, I spent months working for a miser, wearing uncomfortable woolen Victorian garb, and carrying my nephew Robin (who played Tiny Tim) on my shoulder. For this, I got no money, a rash, and a very sore shoulder, and that's the way I played the part. To play the equally challenging role of Captain Smollett, I worked on a boat for half a year and enjoyed every moment of it, though I did learn that getting that little boat into the bottle is a whole lot tougher than it looks. Unlike me, my fellow Muppets took a more naturalistic approach to playing their parts, which is a nice way of saying they just showed up.

Getting back to being ourselves on the big screen, we then made a movie called *Muppets from Space*, an incredible story about Gonzo, filled with astonishing stunts, epic interstellar philosophical musings, and, of course, several catchy musical numbers.

Finally, after years of struggling, then becoming overnight sensations, The Muppets were established members of the Hollywood community. Needless to say, the Hollywood community had no idea how we got in, but we were there, and there was no getting rid of us.

We went on to make a few TV show, specials, and films that showcased

*Note to fact checker: I don't remember any begging. Come to think of it, I don't remember meeting either of these writers. Please verify before publication. —K the F

*I'm a frog of many faces!*

our love of theme parks, our love of holidays, and even our love of yellow brick roads. Little did we know the future was going to get even brighter!

## How to Break the Internet

The Muppets have always been pioneers, bravely going where no frogs, pigs, and bears have gone before. Having made movies and television shows was great, but we were ready to try something new. And where better for a web-footed frog to make his mark than on the Internet?

Even today, no one is certain how the Internet works. (I asked Dr. Honeydew and Beaker to look into it, but last I heard they were still having trouble figuring out how to turn on the computer.) But not knowing how stuff works and diving in anyway is what The Muppets do best. So, we started making viral videos. Okay, so we didn't set out to make them viral, and yet viral they became.

Folks around the world, millions and millions, flocked to their computers to watch the videos we made. Shock! Awe! Disbelief! And even the occasional guffaw! What began as a simple video conference call turned into our biggest online sensation. Inspired by the classic Queen rock song and starring virtually every Muppet known, The Muppets' "Bohemian Rhapsody" introduced us to a whole new generation of web surfers with way too much time on their hands. Millions around the world have watched this video, and while no one can quite figure out what it all means, everyone agrees that it's one of our most mesmerizing creations.

And yet, as much as I love appearing on laptops and desktops worldwide, I knew it was time for us to get back up on the big screen again. One problem: What to name the movie? We kicked around lots of titles, and lots of titles kicked us around, but nothing seemed to capture the spirit of this new picture. And then, after falling asleep at my desk in my office one night, I woke with a start!

"*The Muppets!*" I called out.

Immediately, all of The Muppets came running, making for one extremely crowded office.

"*The Muppets!*" I said again.

Everyone kind of stared at me, hemming, hawing, and shuffling their feet awkwardly.

"What are *vous* talking about?" asked Miss Piggy with her trademark candor and complete lack of patience.

"*The Muppets,*" I said a third time. "That's the title for our new movie!"

Almost everyone loved the idea, except for Pepé the King Prawn, who thought it might be better to just call our movie "The," in the hope of confusing people into buying tickets just to find out what that title meant. Overcoming Pepé's objections (by cutting him in on a share of the gross), it was settled: Our new movie would be called *The Muppets*.

And it was our biggest hit ever! Audiences cheered! The critics loved it! Except, of course, for Statler and Waldorf, who didn't like the fact that there were Muppets in the movie. You can't please all of the people all of the time, and you can't please those two guys ever.

*The Muppets* was our first theatrical release in over a decade, and making it meant that we got the whole gang back together on a film set again. Miss Piggy loved the fact that she got to play a Paris fashion editor in the movie. She spent a year researching the role, mostly by going to Paris, buying clothes, eating rich French pastry . . . and then charging it all to the production. Gonzo loved playing the head of a toilet emporium, truly the pinnacle of success for a blue weirdo who started out as a solo plumber. And Walter loved the fact that he got to meet all of us Muppets, and then was flabbergasted when he realized he also had to be in the movie with us.

We all had so much fun making *The Muppets* that we figured we'd do it again. In fact, there was a while when the sequel to *The Muppets* was called *The Muppets Again*, but the very intelligent folks in research thought that *The Muppets: Most Wanted* was more intriguing. More elusive. More mysterious. Y'know, now that I think about it, I suspect Pepé had a hand in that title, as well. . . .

*The Muppets: Most Wanted* had us all over Europe, singing, dancing, and (for some of us) being impersonated by a green impersonator. Sure, there were long days and nights filming the movie, but we were surrounded by incredible guest stars and incredible landmarks. Sometimes you just gotta scratch your head and wonder how a frog from the swamps made it all the way in front of a camera at the Tower of London, surrounded by his closest friends.

Hot off the heels of *The Muppets: Most Wanted*, we broke into the coveted prime-time-television-and-theme-park-restaurant status that every tadpole dreams of. We pushed the limits on capitalization and punctuation with a TV series called *the muppets*, and Rizzo the Rat opened a brand-new Italian restaurant called PizzeRizzo at the Walt Disney World Resort.

I guess that reminds me. Remember that guy Jim Henson that I met back in Washington, DC? Well, he had this wacky dream that The Muppets should do a project at a Disney theme park. So somewhere in between *The Muppets Take Manhattan* and *The Muppet Christmas Carol*, when Jim wasn't playing with crystals or solving mazes, he managed to get us all together to work on a fancy special effects movie for the Walt Disney World Resort called *Muppet\*Vision 3D*. We kept it very classy, never stooping to cheap 3D tricks or anything. It even had a glorious fireworks finale thanks to Sam Eagle! The folks at the Walt Disney World Resort even decided to give Sam Eagle his own American barbecue restaurant at EPCOT. And then they offered Bunsen and Beaker a scientifically seasonal hot wing location! Between the Regal Eagle Smokehouse and Brew-Wing Lab, it seems like there are no culinary heights that can't be scaled by The Muppets. (Just, uh, don't tell the Swedish Chef that everyone else has restaurants, okay?)

Before we knew it, the entertainment landscape began to change. But luckily for us Muppets, we handle change exceptionally well. People started to "cut the cord" on cable and turn their attention to streaming services. And who knows more about streams than a frog? We dipped our toe in the water with a limited series called *Muppets Now*, which was completed and released during a particularly tough time in the world. It showcased The Muppets each doing what we each do best—Miss Piggy giving lifestyle tips, the Swedish Chef hosting cooking competitions, Pepé doing . . . whatever it is that a shellfish-slash-game-show-host would do.

It turned out that making content for a streaming platform wasn't as scary as we thought. Unfortunately, Gonzo overheard me say that and thought he could prove me wrong. So Gonzo and Pepé put their heads together to figure out how to make our first-ever Halloween special. Despite countless holiday season TV appearances, shows, and specials over the years, somehow we'd never gotten around to making a Halloween special. We started with the important questions: How scary could it be? How silly could it be? And then it hit us. (Metaphorically, of course. Gonzo has assured me ghosts can't make physical contact with the living.) The folks at Walt Disney Imagineering had already solved that balance of scary and silly in their Haunted Mansion attractions, beloved around the world. Thus was born our first Halloween special: *Muppets Haunted Mansion*. Gonzo and Pepé got to play around with all the illusions and special effects, and the rest of us Muppets got to take on iconic characters from the attractions. Fozzie would play the Hatbox Ghost, Miss Piggy would take on the role of Madame Leota, and even Statler and Waldorf got in on the spooky shenanigans, filming a scene in an actual Doom Buggy we borrowed from Disneyland Park.

But we didn't stop there. Somewhere along the way, we realized that Dr. Teeth, Floyd, Janice, Lips, Zoot, and Animal had been making music with us since *The Muppet Show*, but had never gotten around to recording an album. So while the band finally sat down and made a record, we also got the folks in streaming to make them a series. *The Muppets Mayhem* loosely followed the events of recording the album, in the same kind-of-sort-of-loosely way that *The Muppet Movie* followed the events of getting our big break in Hollywood. I wasn't in it, but it was a lot of fun to see all the fans celebrate The Electric Mayhem. And for Animal to finally have some spare vinyl records to snack on.

# CHAPTER

4

# Still a Tadpole with Dreams

**B**eing able to entertain people and make a living doing it is a dream come true. And while spending every single day in the company of a wonderfully dysfunctional band of crazies may not have originally been part of my dream, it's made that dream so much better.

## Hollywood & Beyond

Through it all, I've tried to make sure that success didn't spoil the frog. Y'see, deep down, I'm still that frog from the swamp, the one who started out as not much more than a head and a tail and a wish to make the world smile. I want to be treated like Kermit the Frog, not Kermit the Star. Sometimes, when I walk into a room, people try to treat me as if I were big like a mountain or important like an ocean or tall like a tree (okay, maybe not tall), when the fact is I'm as cool and friendly as ever.

That kind of treatment can go to your head. Some folks in Hollywood don't know how to handle success—the accolades, kudos, awards, backslapping, and "I-loved-your-last-movie-sweetie-baby" flattery that's so common around Tinseltown. Of course, some folks thrive on that kind of treatment; that's one of the things I've always admired about Miss Piggy. That pig really knows how to wallow in her perks.

Not me. As much as I want to stand in the spotlight and make people laugh, when the spotlight goes off I just want to be one of the frogs. To this day, I'm still a bit nervous when I first step into a spotlight. (I guess it reminds me of a bad incident involving a dirt road and a car with one headlight.)

So, how does one stay humble in Hollywood? Well, I guess it's as simple as the story I've just told you. Y'see, I've never forgotten that I'm still Mom and Dad the Frog's little boy, a tadpole with a dream in his heart, a song in his voice, and a sometimes-painful banjo on his knee.

I know that deep down inside, we are who we are. And as long as we remain true to our best selves, we can't go wrong. The goodness is there; we just have to believe it, embrace it, and share it with others.

It doesn't matter if you're a frog or a pig or a bear or even a person. It doesn't matter if you're a big fish in a little pond or a small fish in a big pond— you're you, and you matter. And before you know it, you're right where you belong.

I've got a lot I still want to do with my life, but I've learned a lot of lessons so far, and sharing those lessons is one of the reasons I wrote this book in the first place. I hope what I have to say here inspires you.

So there it is: my life so far. What does it all mean? And how can it help you? To find out, read on!

# PART 2
## Lessons
### for Your
## Life

**Self-help.** I never really understood what that term means.

Anything that I've done in my life, I've done with a lot of help from family, friends, fans—even foes. We all need help to dive into the deep end of life and swim to the farthest shore. That's what this part of the book is all about. Don't think of it as self-help; think of it as a web-footed water wing that can help you glide through the surf on your way to where you're going. Wherever you're headed and whoever you want to be, there's something in this section for you:

If you're starting a first job or about to retire somewhere warm and muggy, I've got ideas, advice, and some nice swampland you might be interested in.

If you're graduating, cogitating, perambulating, or just itching for something new to do, look inside and learn more about my own flying leap into life.

If you want advice on dealing with those pigs, bears, and hecklers who surround you, here's a chance to learn from someone who has been there.

If you're trying to find peace inside of you or trying to make the world a more peaceful place for everyone, all I am saying is give the frog a chance.

Most important of all: Whatever you want to do in life, do it. Look for your own Rainbow Connection and never, ever give up.

After all, if a frog can make it, so can you.

CHAPTER

5

# Using Dreams to Set Goals

I t always starts with a dream. When I first decided I wanted to break into show business, I was dreaming. When Fozzie Bear first devoted his life to becoming the world's greatest stand-up comedy bear, he was dreaming. When Gonzo declared that he would launch himself from a giant slingshot into a tub of tapioca pudding, he was dreaming, too. The point is that all of our journeys begin with dreams, with setting goals for where we want to go and who we want to be.

## Setting Goals for Your Life

Every dream is unique. Some dreams are high-reaching, wide-open, castle-in-the-cloud kind of dreams. They're not really about some thing or some place, but rather are about an indefinable sense of longing that fills us with hope for better days to come.

Other dreams are very specific, with itemized descriptions of size, shape, color, model number, square footage, accessories, and tech support. These fill us with a sense of longing, too.

> **The truth is, we each need to dream up our own dreams. You must look deep inside your heart and ask yourself what you really want.**

Whichever the case, this much is clear: You need a dream. But where does one get dreams?

This is no Dreamers' Wholesale Warehouse.

Some people get their dreams when they sleep. But this is a hit-or-miss proposition at best. Sometimes you have an epiphany that reveals in which direction you should be heading. But too often you dream about being dressed as a Mountie and getting chased across a landscape of toasters by a hippo singing show tunes.

Perhaps the nearest we've come to making it easier to find your dream is a device developed by Muppet Labs: the high-speed iDream player, which allows you to download digital dreams off the Internet. (Early tests were promising; then Beaker began to develop a severe case of spontaneous combustion. Dr. Honeydew wisely went back to the drawing board, while Beaker warily spent some time with the local bomb squad.)

The truth is, we each need to dream up our own dreams. You must look deep inside your heart and ask yourself what you really want.

Finding your dream is a solitary endeavor. So what can a frog do to help?

Well, it is tempting to wish you the best and move along to other pressing questions, like "Why are there so many songs about rainbows?" "How does cold fusion work?" and "Where can I hide from a show-tune singing hippo?"

But I wouldn't do that to you, especially when I just happen to have a seven-step system that will allow you to identify, locate, and settle on your very own life's dream. Whether this is your first hop into the watery depths of dreaming or you're already all wet, this exercise should help you make a big splash. Let's dive in!

# I.
## Your Foundations: Inner Dreams

Inner Dreams are your very first dreams. They are the dreams you have when you're a tadpole swimming around the rocks and wondering "What's a rock?" and "Should I talk to it?" and "Gee, I wonder why that rock isn't talking to me." For people of the human species, it's the dream you have when you're lying on your back in your crib looking at all those big faces making moon-eyes at you, which you ponder wordlessly to yourself: "Who are these people? And why do they keep looking at me and making odd noises?"

Inner Dreams are about answering the three most fundamental questions of life: Who am I? Where am I? And how the heck did I get here? In short (and I sure am), Inner Dreams are all about defining yourself. Oh sure, dreaming that "I'm a frog in the swamp and I got here by water" may seem like a simple dream right now. But it's the foundation for everything that comes later in life.

For instance, if Statler and Waldorf hadn't defined themselves early on as curmudgeons, Fozzie Bear might have been spared years of hurled invectives and tossed tomatoes. If Animal hadn't first defined himself as the world's loudest drummer, some of us might still have our hearing.

And if Bean Bunny hadn't first defined himself as adorable beyond comprehension, all of us would have to try a lot harder to convince audiences that Muppets could be cute.

Most of you reading this have probably already had these Inner Dreams. Chances are you already know who you are, where you are, and how you got there.

The most important part of these

*I look pretty "dreamy," right?!*

Inner Dreams is that they are your dreams. It's important that you don't let outer dreams and dreamers define you. These days, it's too easy to borrow someone else's dream. Who wouldn't want to be that woman singing her heart out on social media or that basketball star sinking a three-pointer to win the game or that very hairy guy with way too many tattoos who built a houseboat out of beef jerky? (Okay, you may want to take a pass on that last one.)

There's something extremely tempting about co-opting other people's dreams. All the work is done for you. I was the same way when I was young; I had turtle dreams. Hey, who wouldn't want a shell like that? It is like your own air-conditioned customized van with a high-gloss airbrushed exterior, knee-deep shag-carpeted interior, and four on the floor. I wasn't alone.

Fortunately, I outgrew that dream, came out of my shell, and embraced the dream of being the best frog I could be. Once you've reached this point and figured out who you are, it's time to move on to . . .

# 2.
## Your Explorations: Outer Dreams

This is the fun part. The Outer Dream is where you move beyond defining who you are and start figuring out who you might want to be by trying on different dreams. This is more commonly known as playing dress-up.

Kids are the true experts at Outer Dreaming. They just love to try on different dreams. Who hasn't heard a young tadpole announce that they really want to be an astronaut, a fashion designer, a doctor, a diva, an artist, a puppet, a pauper, a pirate, a poet, a pawn, and a king . . . all at the same time, of course.

Pigs don't just tell you what they want to be—they make sure you get them all the necessary accoutrements and accessories to make their dreams a reality.

Others, however, are not comfortable with Outer Dreaming. They settle on their Inner Dream and never let go.

Take Sam Eagle, who strictly forbids himself from dreaming about being anything other than an unwavering patriot who is appalled at, well, everything. The same goes for Dr. Bunsen Honeydew, a born scientist who had great difficulty dreaming of any future that didn't involve a lab coat, test tubes, and things that smell of sulfur. And needless to say, Beaker never considered any dream beyond being a loyal scientific assistant and victim of science experiments gone wrong.

If you're ready to Outer Dream, I personally recommend the daily dream method. This allows you to try on a wide variety of dreams without having to constantly change clothes during the day.

Enjoy Outer Dreaming. It's your chance to sample what the world has to offer. As the Swedish Chef says:

 **Tastée de smørgasbrøød øøf life! Yøø betcha!**

**One word of warning: Outer Dreaming can be habit-forming. Some people so enjoy trying on different dreams that they never settle on a single goal in life—an affliction that commonly leads to whopping college tuition bills.**

## 3.
### Your Ambitions: Big Dreams

"Hey, World! I'm Kermit the Frog and I'm gonna be a star!" If you were walking by a swamp and heard someone shout this out, you'd probably have one of three reactions:

"Cool, a talking frog."

"Yipes! Not another Kermit impersonator!"

"Yeah, right!"

Well, when I was a young frog and stood in the middle of the swamp shouting out those very words, the reaction was unanimously: "Yeah, right!" Almost no one believed in me. Okay, my mom and dad were encouraging, even going so far as to sign me up for tap-dancing lessons and a one-year subscription to *Wannabe Magazine*. But, by and large, the world reacted with a big yawn.

Expect the same. When you decide what your Big Dream is, you'll be bursting with enthusiasm and want to share it with everybody. Here's what will happen. Most everybody will give you one of those "Okay, that's nice, now please pass the ketchup" looks. Some will scoff, suggesting that whatever your Big Dream is, it's too big for you. And a select few will whisper words of encouragement.

My advice is this: Pass the ketchup. Ignore the scoffers. And remember those words of encouragement, 'cause they're the only ones that matter.

I always try to be encouraging. No matter who comes to me with their talent or dream, I try to find something positive to say. Sometimes this can be tough, but it's always worth the effort.

Take Lew Zealand. He came to us with a very Big Dream—to be the world's best boomerang fish thrower. (Seeing as he was already the world's only boomerang fish thrower, this dream was well within reach.) At first I said to myself: Do we really need a boomerang fish thrower? But throwing caution to the wind, I said yes, and the rest is history. Where would The Muppets be today without Lew Zealand and His Boomerang Fish? I don't know, but we'd be ducking airborne haddock a lot less, that's for sure.

The same goes for Fozzie Bear, whose Big Dream is being a great stand-up comic. Fozzie's act didn't get laughs, but his dream did. And that's when he came to me, and I told him: "You can do it, Fozzie. I believe in you." Gee, it seems like only yesterday I said that. (Come to think of it, it was only yesterday; Fozzie is one very insecure bear.)

The point is, we have to appreciate and encourage others' dreams. Then, if we're lucky, someone will encourage ours.

# 4.
## Your Strategy: Little Dreams

There's an old saying in my family: "You can't cross the whole swamp in one big leap." You have to take each trip one hop at a time. Oh, and always avoid moving rocks because these tend to be hungry alligators with an appetite for amphibians.

The point is that every Big Dream is made up of Little Dreams. If you take the time to achieve each Little Dream, before you know it your Big Dreams will be within reach. This may seem like reasonable and easy-to-follow advice, but when you want something as much as we all want our Big Dream, it's very tempting to try to accomplish it all at once.

Everyone wants to be an overnight success, but this rarely happens. Oh sure, some seem to achieve instant success. Just look at Pepé the King Prawn. He started out in the ocean as one of several million prawns. Then all of a sudden, he went from a net cast off the coast of Spain to being a part of our cast in movies and on television. A meteoric rise, for sure. But his success wasn't really that easy. Pepé still had to strive and struggle to get where he is today. True, most of his striving involved shameless wheedling, scamming, and outright fibbing, but he still did it one duplicitous step at a time.

I'm not recommending that you follow Pepé's particular path, but it is important to break down your dream into doable parts. For me, with my dream of Hollywood stardom, I had to first master such smaller dreams as dancing, singing, banjo playing, acting, and, of course, schmoozing.

So break down your Big Dream and Little Dreams, and then go after each with all the gusto you can muster! And whatever you do, stay away from those moving rocks.

# 5.

## Your Insecurities: Faltering Dreams

Reality hits! Now I'm not talking about "reality show" reality; I'm talking about real-life reality, the kind that doesn't get resolved in thirty minutes and is interrupted by ads because you refuse to pay more for the premium account.

Real life has a way of altering the best-laid plans. No matter what you started out dreaming, no matter what goals you set at the outset, chances are that life will interfere and cause you to falter.

Look at what happened to Dr. Teeth, whose first dream was to be a classical concert pianist, playing the great compositions of Bach, Beethoven, Mozart, and all those other long-haired dudes. Then reality hit. His parents expected him to take over the family business. After all, he came from a long line of Dr. Teeths renowned for their dental abilities. What was the good doctor to do—give up on music, perish the thought? No way! He grabbed Floyd Pepper, hopped in a bus, and went to make music that would change the world. And thank goodness that he did, otherwise we might not have the tunes of the Electric Mayhem to brighten our lives. Can you picture that?

If your dream hits a snag like this, don't be discouraged, and don't give up. Retreat, regroup, reconnoiter, and prepare for your return in . . .

# 6.
## Your Preparations: Revised Dreams

The Great Gonzo is famous for saying:

> **That which doesn't kill us makes us stronger, even as it exponentially increases our health insurance premiums.**

In other words, everything that happens has a good and bad side. If you shoot yourself out of a cannon into a tank of angry electric eels, you're going to come out with hair like Beaker's. But you'll never need another night-light for as long as you live. If you cover your body in chopped liver and recite poetry, you're going to have a tough time drawing a crowd, but a pretty darn good chance of getting a government arts grant. Sometimes you can get creative and turn your setback into your next great opportunity!

So it is with dreams. When reality strikes them down, it doesn't mean they're over. It means that you need to figure out what it will take to make them happen.

The Revised Dream is a time of waiting, a time when you hold out hope and prepare for what comes next. A perfect example of this is Miss Piggy. As she made her rise to the top, she found herself in the role of chorus pig. Sure she wanted to be a big star, but fate had placed her in the back row, singing backup. Did she give up? Did she turn back, satisfied with almost making it? Not a chance. The pig stayed in the picture until an opportunity presented itself. And when that opportunity finally appeared, she grabbed it with gusto!

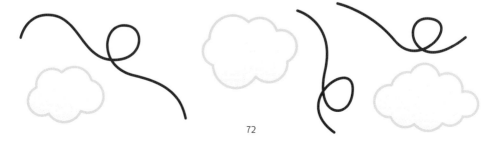

# 7.

## Your Reward: Realized Dreams

When you get to the Realized Dream, the biggest surprise is that it probably doesn't look anything like that goal you had in mind way back when you started. It's different. And yet, somehow, it's even better than you imagined.

I wanted to be in entertainment, a frog who made people happy, but in my wildest dreams I never thought I'd be doing that in the company of Miss Piggy, Fozzie, Gonzo, and the rest. But there they are, and now I can't picture my life any other way.

But the very best part of realizing your dream is knowing that you don't have to stop dreaming or sharing your dream with others.

Dreams are how we figure out where we want to go. Life is how we get there.

# CHAPTER

6

# Leaping Off Your Lily Pad

**W**hether you just sprouted legs or left your tail behind a very long time ago, one thing is certain: You'll probably need a push to get started. Having dreams and setting goals is important, but nothing is going to happen if you sit around. You need to get off your tail, leap off your lily pad, and get on with it!

# Leading a Most Sensational, Inspirational, Motivational Life

Consider me your short, green, personal motivational coach, here to help you confront your fears, overcome your doubts, release your potential, and tidy up afterward. Ready? I'll be right with you; I need to get my whistle and clipboard.

## A Farewell to Fears

The first step is to admit that you have fears and doubts. Don't be shy. Everyone has them, even the indomitable and seemingly fearless Miss Piggy. To this day she still fears that she won't get enough attention in the media and doubts that the Academy will finally come to its senses and give her an award. (She would like me to specify that she is not referring to "one of those hinky-dink Lifetime Achievement Awards." She wants the real, golden ones.)

Miss Piggy has confronted her fears and doubts—and even optioned them as a possible movie. Now it's your turn.

To help you get started, I've compiled a list of the most common fears, and appropriate strategies I've developed for dealing with them.

**Fear of Public Speaking.** I hear about this one from folks a lot. Try picturing an audience full of supportive friends and loved ones. It's a lot easier to talk if you feel like everyone's already on your side.

**Fear of Failure.** If you fail and learn from your failure, you're a success. If you fail to learn from your failure, you are likely to fail again or go to work at Muppet Labs, where failure is not an option—it's what we do best.

**Fear of Making a Fool of Yourself.** Throughout history, all great people have been considered fools in their own time. This doesn't necessarily mean every fool is a great person, but it's reassuring to have history on your side.

**Fear of the Unknown.** I've worked with the unknown my whole life. Trust me: They're a swell bunch, especially Gonzo. (In an earlier edition of this book, "fear of the unknown" was incorrectly listed as "fear of the unicorn." I don't have any advice for that fear, but it is an excellent typo.)

**Fear of Fear Itself.** President Franklin Delano Roosevelt said, "We have nothing to fear but fear itself." It's sometimes easier said than done when you're Rizzo the Rat being asked to perform high-flying special effects stunts in classic Victorian attire. Stop fearing fear and you become fearless. You're ready for anything (as long as you remember where you put your jelly beans).

## Muppet Motivational Strategies

You're finally ready to face life's challenges. This is where all of our motivational prep work comes into play and we truly "Take a Flying Leap!"

What does this phrase mean? Simple. It means that you are committed to being the best frog (or enter your species here) that you can be. You want to face life's challenges with confidence, enthusiasm, and foolhardy abandon!

To help you achieve this, I've developed Muppet Motivational Strategies. With help from the other Muppets, I've come up with answers to many of life's most vexing questions. (And who wants to be vexed, right?)

No matter where you are in life (youth, middle age, old, really old, toast), we have a strategy for you. Let us know if any of them work.

## Strategies for School

**Challenge:** How can I make a good impression on the first day of school?

**Strategy:** Fozzie suggests trying to impersonate Elvis. It's easy to do, and a real crowd-pleaser. Being able to do a good Elvis will not only make you a hit at recess, but repeatedly saying "thenkew, thenkew very much" will surely win you points for politeness.

**Challenge:** The teacher doesn't seem to like me.

**Strategy:** Okay, maybe you shouldn't have been singing Elvis tunes in the middle of the math lesson. Sam Eagle suggests always showing authority the utmost respect and gratitude each and every day. Also patriotism. It may not always work to win over your peers, but it should serve you for teachers and school administrators.

**Challenge:** I'm not "in" with the "in" crowd.

**Strategy:** Miss Piggy suggests forming your own "in" group with you as the only member. To emphasize your exclusivity, always carry a red velvet rope and a clipboard with only your name on it. If you become weary of being alone, Piggy can refer you to a number of reasonably priced entourage rental services, such as Rent-a-Groupie.

**Challenge:** I've been in college for more than a decade and still don't know what I want to study.

**Strategy:** Who said there's anything wrong with studying a little bit of everything? To this day, Gonzo studies stuntwork, plumbing, poultry psychology, and even mycology. Just graduate and consider yourself to be a Muppet.

## Strategies for Work

**Challenge:** My first job interview is tomorrow. How do I ace it?

**Strategy:** There's nothing quite as stress inducing as a job interview. And there's nothing quite so stress relieving as a chat with Rowlf the Dog. Take it from Rowlf: be cool, calm, and collected. Ask interesting questions. And don't forget to give yourself a treat after for a job well done.

**Challenge:** My boss keeps giving all the big assignments and promotions to someone else. How do I get the boss to notice me?

**Strategy:** Floyd Pepper of the Electric Mayhem says, "If the boss doesn't notice you, then you got it made, dude, so just chill." As appealing as big assignments and promotions can seem to the untrained eye, it is Floyd's experience that these actually result in "heavy lifting and most unrighteous headaches." He suggests a "stealth employee" approach to work. You're on the payroll, but otherwise you're flying under the radar. Come to think of it, I haven't seen Floyd since payday.

**Challenge:** I don't want to be a "stealth employee." I'm a hard-charging, type-A personality. Any other suggestions?

**Strategy:** Get a job working near Floyd. You'll look positively turbocharged by comparison. Of course, this means you first have to find Floyd.

**Challenge:** I'm tired of the corporate world and want to start my own business. What should I do to leave the rat race?

**Strategy:** Try Hollywood, suggests Rizzo the Rat, our expert on rat-race exit strategies. No one here has a clue about what they're doing or what anyone else is supposed to be doing. Rizzo's personal career suggestion? "Be a producer. You don't have to act, write, or direct; all youse got to do is ask people for money. Heck, I been a producer for years!"

**Challenge:** I'm torn between wanting to put in more hours at work and spending more time with my family. What can I do?

**Strategy:** I have this same difficulty, which is why I turned to Dr. Bunsen Honeydew, who suggests the Muppet Labs Send-in-the-Clones 3000. It's fun, efficient, and easy to operate. Just ask Beaker. And Beaker. And Beaker. And Beaker. And Beaker. And Beaker. And Beaker. And Beaker.

## Strategies for the Golden Years

**Challenge:** I'm just beginning my retirement. How can I make the most of my newfound free time?

**Strategy:** Our resident retirement experts, Statler and Waldorf, suggest that you take up a hobby.

**Complaining is our favorite. You meet lots of new people.**

**Yeah, and you get to annoy the bejabbers out of them!**

Pretty soon you'll be moving on to related activities, like the menacing glare, talking too loud at the movies, and the ever-popular dousing those pesky kids with the garden hose.

**Challenge:** What's the best way to stay healthy in my later years?

**Strategy:** According to Statler: "Don't get old." But according to Pops, getting a part-time gig at a place you enjoy working is a nice way to stay active after retirement, too.

**Challenge:** My children don't appreciate all that I've done for them over the years. How can I get them to show their gratitude?

**Strategy:** Leave it to Waldorf. "Where there's a last will, there's a way!" Good grief.

CHAPTER

7

# Muppet
# Money
# Management

**M**oney is not a big issue with frogs. It may not be easy being green, but when it comes to managing the green stuff, my attitude is "easy come, easy go." Hey, when you have sunshine, blue skies, flies around your head, and the peaceful sounds of nature all around, what more could you possibly want?

## Managing Your Green

Over the years I've had to learn the basics of handling money. For instance, I needed a safe and convenient place to put cash. (This is one of the disadvantages of not having pockets . . . or pants, usually.) Through trial and error I discovered that between the couch cushions is an ideal place to store cash reserves, as well as broken pretzels, half-eaten donuts, and other valuable assets.

It's one thing to deal with your own money, but a whole other thing to manage other people's money. When The Muppets decided to launch our show, someone had to take on fiduciary responsibility. (This is a technical financial term that defines the relationship between a trustee and the money held in trust; it basically means that if we run out of money, someone goes to jail.) Because no one else was willing to do hard time, I was elected as the responsible one.

> **It's one thing to deal with your own money, but a whole other thing to manage other people's money.**

With the help of our board of directors (aka The Muppet Thursday Night Canasta Poker and Kickboxing Club), we devised a financial strategy that would enable us to put on a high-quality, high-budget television variety show. Now I could go into great detail about the various fiscal mechanisms utilized, but suffice it to say that we basically operated under the time-honored system of endless borrowing.

Before long we were piling up an enormous debt. However, when it became clear that we couldn't raise taxes the way the government does, it was time to move to the next chapter of our financial plan, better known as Chapter II.

That's when I turned to the Bank of Amphibia. ("Our Assets Are Always Liquid.") From their overflowing cash flow to their renowned deal-making abilities, these are the finest minds in business. Almost everyone has heard of their most famous transaction—the Great Swampland Sale—where millions of dollars were sunk into a development that, much to everyone's surprise, became the state of Florida. With a record like that, and no place else to turn, we decided to trust the Bank of Amphibia with all of The Muppets' financial dealings.

Has it worked out? Who knows? No matter how many times I update the Bank of Amphibia app, it always give me the loading screen, but never actually lets me log in.

But that's okay because all this time waiting has taught me two things:

First, if I watch that little lily pad spin in a circle one more time, I'm going to throw my phone across the room!

Second, whether you're high income, low income, or no income, you need to take control of your own financial future.

And so, with the help of my fellow Muppets, I've put together a list of everything you need to know about money. Or at least everything that we know about money. Although these philosophical insights may not help you save and invest, or become a billionaire, they can make you more comfortable with whatever cash you already happen to have. And unlike every other financial guide, they won't make you lose any money. Unless, of course, you happen to go shoe shopping with Miss Piggy.

# Our Money Manual

**According to Piggy: Too Much Is Never Enough.** This is Miss Piggy's foremost rule about money. And for that matter, her rule about shoes, food, jewelry, publicity, designer dresses, awards . . . and everything else in life. Admittedly, this doesn't help you get money, unless of course you're Miss Piggy, who has a knack for getting other people to pay for stuff.

**According to Rizzo the Rat: Cryptocurrency Is Not Physical Money.** This discovery was made by Rizzo's second cousin, Iggy, on an ill-fated attempt to cash in on a growing investment craze. Following in the footsteps of Cousin Blinky (still serving time in Rattica Prison), Iggy tried to mint his own bills and pass them off as cryptocurrency . . . not realizing, of course, that cryptocurrency is entirely digital. (And that the bills do not, in fact, feature illustrations of crypts.) The lesson remains that counterfeiting is not the greatest way to make money.

*Rizzo the Rat's cousin's currency.*

**According to Muppet Labs: Money Does Not Grow on Trees.** Despite repeated efforts in the little understood field of Arboreal Currency Creation, Dr. Bunsen Honeydew and Beaker of Muppet Labs have yet to successfully produce an oak that grows C-notes, a bougainvillea that blooms ten-spots, or an evergreen that is, indeed, ever green.

**According to Swedish Chef: If You Need Dough, Raise Dough.** Or, more authentically: "Yøø kneédeé de døøgh tu råzeé de døøgh! Børk! Børk! Børk!" According to our noted in-house punologist, Dr. Bob of Veterinarian's Hospital, this appears to be a bad baking pun related to kneading dough. If you need to know more about this Swedish take on money, see Dr. Bob for translation assistance.

**According to Sam Eagle: Money Is the Root of All Evil.** Noted authority on all things inappropriate, Sam Eagle states unequivocally that money is the cause of all that is wrong with the world, including but not limited to indecency, insubordination, lack of manners, and those annoying pop-up ads in the middle of his patriotic live streams. However, upon discovering that pictures of the presidents of the United States of America were to be found on U.S. currency, Sam recently modified his pronouncement with the following terse addendum: "Never mind."

**According to Pepé the King Prawn: Real Wealth Is Not About Money.** This bit of advice was surprising, given the source. According to Pepé, real wealth comes from being with the people you love. That's awfully nice! Oh wait. There's more to it. "Real wealth comes from being with the people you love . . . then borrowing the money they have. Because love means never having to pay them back." Ah. There it is.

**According to Statler and Waldorf: You Can't Take It With You. (But You Can Sure as Heck Try.)** The internationally renowned curmudgeons have accumulated a vast fortune over a lifetime of heckling and complaining. (Apparently people pay a lot of money to make them leave. Wouldn't you?) They are determined to succeed in squandering every last cent before exiting

the balcony for the last time. "Where there's a will, there's a way," says Statler. "And where there's a last will, there are lots of no-good relatives."

**According to the Electric Mayhem: Money Can't Buy You Love.** Not surprisingly, the band experienced this group epiphany while listening to a Beatles album. Either way, the Mayhem had no money, so it wasn't a big deal.

**According to Fozzie Bear: Money Is Funny.** Our resident comedian would like to offer up the following example:

> **Why did the chicken cross the Wall Street? Cause that's where she laid her nest egg! Wocka wocka!**

I suggest that Fozzie invest in some new material. It only makes cents. Yipes, I think Fozzie's jokes are contagious!

If you ask me—and you're reading this book, so I'm assuming you're open to my advice—our true worth is measured by what we give, not what we have. The only time that money does any good is when we share it with others to make their lives a little better. Oh sure, we all need to take care of ourselves, but if we become obsessed with money, it starts to own us. Pretty soon we're the ones who feel locked in a vault, separated from the happiness that friendship and sharing can bring.

Just think of Ebenezer Scrooge. Despite his wealth, he wasn't a happy man. But when he gave freely of himself, he got back much more in return. I've been blessed with success and friendship with friends who are more than willing to share whatever I'm willing to give them. I hope you are, too.

CHAPTER

8

# Expecting the Unexpected

**W**hen people look at my life, they usually focus on the highlights. They see the television shows and movies I've done, the big stars I've had the opportunity to work with, and all the other trappings that go with living in Hollywood. I guess that's okay. After all, people like to talk about accomplishments. But we all know that life is more than an endless series of great moments. Everyone faces setbacks: difficult tasks, disappointing results, and the occasional karate chop from an angry pig. We wish these things wouldn't happen, but they do. We wish we could forget all about them, but we can't.

## Taking on Tough Times

Bad things happen to everyone, even to good frogs. For centuries great philosophers, theologians, and game show runners-up have puzzled over this conundrum. They have developed grand theories, written scholarly texts, complained to the judges, and gone home with lousy consolation prizes. But they've never really answered the questions we really want answered:

> **Why do bad things happen?**
> **What can we do once they happen to us?**

What makes me think that a mere frog can answer profound questions that have stymied the greatest minds in history? I realized that although the greatest minds may have tackled this topic, it's never been wrestled to the ground and analyzed by that uniquely skewed intellectual collective known as The Muppets. So I recently brought together several of our most brilliant and available minds, each with its own peculiar take on why bad things happen and what you can do about it.

I asked Dr. Bunsen Honeydew of Muppet Labs, representing the scientific opinion; Miss Piggy, representing the diva worldview; and Sgt. Floyd Pepper, representing himself. Oh, and when I was conducting interviews, Pepé the King Prawn showed up, too. Here's what they had to say:

**Dr. Bunsen Honeydew, ESQ:** You see, Beaker and I have developed several theorems and a variety of formulae related to negative occurrence and its impact on experientiality. The first reason that bad things happen is "by accident." The second school of thought is that they occur "on purpose." A malevolent force acting upon an undeserving object creates a distinctly unpleasant causal relationship. The results are inconclusive. We'll find more funding to further our research.

**Miss Piggy:** If something bad happens to *vous*, just sue them! Any diva worth her press clippings simply adores a good legal battle. It can keep *vous* in the tabloids and on those TV entertainment shows for months!

**Sgt. Floyd Pepper:** When bad things happen to me, I write songs about 'em. That's how I got some of my biggest hits.

Editor's note: Pepé didn't really contribute anything of substance to the conversation, but he did make a passing comment about using a bad situation as an opportunity to "make monies."

I guess this leads me to my point: Don't just expect the unexpected, see how you can use it.

Some, like Dr. Honeydew, are curious and eager to learn more. Some, like Pepé, are opportunistic, doing their best to turn a negative into a positive. Some, like Miss Piggy, are willing to fight back—or to hire someone who charges by the hour to fight back for them. A lucky few, like Floyd, aren't quite sure what happened and won't remember it afterward, so what difference does it make anyway? But, for many like myself, the only way to deal with difficult times is to accept them and learn from the experience. And what have I learned? I'm so glad you asked, because I just happen to have an entire section devoted to this topic!

# What I've Learned About Bad Things

**Bad Things Hurt.** Sometimes the hurt is physical, as when Gonzo misjudges his motorcycle reentry trajectory and lands on your instep or when Sweetums knocks you over as he sprints to Free Pretzel Day. Sometimes the hurt goes deeper, as when someone disappoints you or Sweetums lands on your instep. In either case, you must try to heal. Let time pass and the hurt will go away, though you may walk with a limp.

**Bad Things Don't Mean Bad People.** We are all capable of causing bad things to happen to others; that does not mean we are bad. Even when someone goes out of their way to make bad things happen to people, that doesn't mean they are bad. We have to give people the benefit of the doubt and to forgive them for the hurt they may cause.

**Attitude Is Everything.** There are two ways to react to bad things. The easy way is to get angry, cast aspersions, and generally get in a bad mood about the world and everything in it. For an advanced course in this approach, see Statler and Waldorf's classic guide on curmudgeonliness, *How We Learned to Stop Worrying and Start Blaming You*. The other way to react takes a lot more work: You can get over it. That's right; accept it, be happy you survived it, and get past it. Then make every effort to prevent bad things from happening to you and to others. (This includes not standing too close to Statler and Waldorf.)

**Why Worry?** The only thing worse than having something bad happen to you is worrying about it beforehand. Constant fretting can make you afraid to face the world or even get up in the morning. Worrying doesn't do anything to actually solve the problem, but it does a heck of a job of adding to your stress.

**If It Were Easy, Everyone Would Be You.** Overcoming difficult times is what turns you into "you." Let's be honest, I wouldn't be me—for better or worse—if it didn't take me so long to break into show business. Fozzie wouldn't be Fozzie if it weren't for the long, hard trek he has made in his rise to the comedic heights, relatively speaking. And who would Gonzo be if it weren't for his constant violations of the laws of gravity, aerodynamics, and common sense? We are often at our best when we're facing our worst situations. Know that when you come out of it, you can be a better you.

> **Life is great. But without bad times, we wouldn't know the difference.**

**Life Is Great.** But without bad times, we wouldn't know the difference.

# CHAPTER

# 9

# DEALING
## with
## Difficult Personalities

*I'm no therapist. But when it comes to dealing with people—and various other species—I know my stuff. Most of the folks I've met in life have been very kind, extremely generous, and not afraid to get their feet wet working with a frog. But I've also had to spend time with some really difficult personalities. I know that dealing with difficult personalities is part of everyone's life. It has always been a part of my life, that's for sure. Whether you have to deal with pigs and divas (or pigs who are divas) or just your everyday, run-of-the-mill, pain-in-the-neck person, you need ways to make the experience less painful, more productive, and less likely to result in your head exploding. (Believe me, it happens all the time where I work.)*

## It's Easy Being Mean

Grumbling, griping, groaning, and grousing come naturally to everyone. We all can be difficult at times. And don't think I'm immune to this just because I'm a bug-eyed green celebrity. (Let's face it: The Incredible Hulk has made a career of losing his temper—and celebrities don't get any more big-eyed and green than

> **Some of us shout. Some pout. Me? I wave my spindly green arms in the air and make high-pitched sounds until I run out of breath.**

he does.) Sometimes the urge to throw a fit—or hurl an SUV across the Grand Canyon—is just irresistible.

For most of us, these angry feelings happen when we find ourselves in a stressful situation. Maybe it happens when someone yells at work or cuts you off as you're driving down the freeway (or, if you're a frog, when they cut you off as you're trying to cross the freeway). Or maybe it happens when the next act that you have booked on your variety show suddenly tells you that they're missing a trombone and you wonder aloud why they would make it all the way to the stage without checking to make sure they had their trombone with them and HOW IS IT POSSIBLE TO JUST LOSE A TROMBONE AND . . . sheesh! Forget it.

Anyone faced with this kind of pressure will snap. Some of us shout. Some pout. Me? I wave my spindly green arms in the air and make high-pitched sounds until I run out of breath. I know it's not terribly fearsome, but it's great for letting off steam. And letting off steam is important and necessary. (I'm not sure, but I believe that holding the steam inside is what makes your head explode.) As long as we let off steam in a way that doesn't harm, annoy, or otherwise scald those around us, it's okay. Being difficult at times is part of what it means to be human—or amphibian, for that matter.

The trouble is that some folks out there seem to thrive on being difficult. It defines who they are and how they make their way through life. They come in all shapes and sizes. Here are a few of the chronically difficult types I've met in my time, and where you're most likely to run across them:

## The Queens of Their Universe

**What They Are:** They are unaware that anyone else exists except to serve them. Everyone around this type of person is expected to bow to her every whim. But no matter how nice you are, it's never enough.

**Where to Find (or Avoid) Them:** These people (and pigs) often live in Hollywood, where such over-the-top histrionics can lead to lots of tabloid coverage and a possible award nomination.

## Grumpy Old Men

**What They Are:** Old and grumpy. They are well-known for not liking anything done by anyone, anywhere, at any time. What they lack in tact, they make up for in the accuracy with which they can hurl invectives and rotten tomatoes.

**Where to Find (or Avoid) Them:** They travel in tandem but usually forgo travel, preferring a balcony perch from which to pass judgment on the world.

## Conniving Rats

**What They Are:** Some of my best friends are rats, so I don't want to cast aspersions on all vermin. But there are a few rodents out there who know how to gnaw their way through the drywall of decency and really make pests of themselves. Oh sure, they may once have had a heart of gold beating beneath their scheming exterior, but chances are they've pawned it and used the proceeds to buy knockoff designer watches that they'll happily sell to you wholesale.

**Where to Find (or Avoid) Them:** Leaving sinking ships.

## Obtuse-Itarians

**What They Are:** They don't mean to be difficult; they are simply being their strange, weird, obtuse, and otherwise contrarian selves. You can admire them for their uniqueness and their eccentric joie de vivre, but sooner or later they are going to drive you crazy. Maybe it will happen when the piano they were juggling falls on your foot or when the boomerang fish they threw flies through the air and whacks you on the back of the head. Whatever these obtuse-itarians do, you won't expect it and you won't believe it.

**Where to Find (or Avoid) Them:** Where you least expect or want them.

Of course this isn't a complete list of difficult personalities, and I'm sure that you can think of others just by looking around the room. These are just the ones I run into most often . . . as in every day

. . . as in right now. Now that we've identified some of the most common types of difficult personalities, the question remains: What can you do to make it easier to live with these people?

# Kermit's Tips for Handling Difficult People

 **I'm writing my book right now. Can you come back later? No, I didn't know we were out of chocolate. Okay, okay, I'll go and get some. Sheesh!**

**Be Agreeable.** Remember, if you agree to go get them chocolate, chances are they'll be a lot more agreeable, too. Even if it's only temporary, it's worth the effort. Plus you'll get a break from them while getting the chocolate.

**Be Firm, But Flexible.** Never give in on issues that are really important to you. But be flexible on the little things, such as going to dinner parties, paying overdue credit card bills, repairing rocket-damaged roofs, et cetera.

**Show Your True Feelings.** If someone is getting you hot under the collar, loosen your collar so that some steam seeps out. This may not make them less disagreeable, but the vapors are really great for your complexion.

**Don't Make Yourself a Target.** I always thought that being green and blending in with things was a bad thing, but then I realized that it's great camouflage when some irate individual is looking to make my life miserable. There's nothing wrong with hiding out and waiting until cooler heads prevail.

**Embrace Other Points of View.** So the world you live in and the folks around you are crazy. A chef is chasing a chicken with a meat cleaver. Someone is chasing a chicken with a bouquet of flowers. And now a chicken is rallying all the other chickens to chase the Swedish Chef, clucking their defiance. It may not be normal, but this is your life, so make yourself at home and go a little crazy, too.

**Tap Into Your Inner Best Self.** It's natural to get upset when someone is being difficult. But I find that when you fight fire with fire, you tend to get burned. And there's nothing worse than extra-crispy frog, believe you me. So I try to visualize my most peaceful self, the kind and wonderful Kermit who resides inside of me. And when I've successfully visualized this perfect frog, I send him out to

deal with the problem. And when that doesn't work, at least I have someone to commiserate and share popcorn with during the debacle.

**Try being happy.** Said another way: It's better to be upbeat than beat up. When people are in a bad mood, the last thing they want to do is hang around with happy people. Kind of a win-win.

These suggestions may not solve all your interpersonal difficulties. If they could, I'd change my name to Dr. Gill and have my own afternoon TV advice show. But they may help you navigate the murky, alligator-infested waters that we all face as we paddle our way through the great swamp of life (pardon the metaphor). Do your best and treat others well, and I guarantee the best is yet to come.

CHAPTER

10

# Your Inner Tadpole

**W**hat is your inner tadpole? There are many different definitions. Some call it your soul or spirit. Others call it your conscience. Others call it that annoying little voice that tells you to laugh even though the last joke that Fozzie told was really not all that funny. Whatever you decide to call it, your inner tadpole is what guides you through the calm streams and raging rapids of life. It is the essence of you.

## Childhood You

Your inner tadpole needs you to care for it. It needs you to say, "Thank you, inner tadpole" and "Hey, inner tadpole, want to play a game of solitaire together?" In other words, your inner tadpole needs to know you care.

Young children, being tadpoles themselves, are very much in touch with their inner tadpoles. Their voice of innocence is the voice of their inner tadpole speaking loud and clear. It is refreshing, bracing, and sometimes embarrassing, but it is always honest.

As we leave childhood and deal with all the crises and chaos that come with being a grown-up, we can lose touch with our inner tadpole. We don't talk to it. We don't call or send a box of candy. We get too busy to listen to our inner tadpole, and as a result, we become what is referred to in Swamp Psychology 101 as an "outer toad."

## Facing Your Outer Toad

You know what I mean. The outer toad personality is always croaking about something dreadful that just happened, is happening right now, or might happen any minute. In good times the outer toad expects the worst; in bad times, it expects things to get even worser (not caring for a moment that "worser" is not even a real word*). Your outer toad requires no care or attention. In fact, it thrives on being ignored. That's just something else to complain about, not that it needs an excuse. The outer toad will never be happy until it is unhappy, and then it's happy and unhappy at the same time, which is not only confusing and contradictory, it makes your head hurt to think about it.

*Dear Editor, my apology for this one. —KtheF

### Are You in Touch with Your Outer Toad?

When bad things happen to good people, do you cheer? ___YES ___NO

Did you like Scrooge better before the ghosts showed up? ___YES ___NO

When people tell you to "Have a nice day!" do you respond "No, thanks"? __YES __NO

If you could be any kind of tree, why would you? ___YES ___NO

Are you fed up with how long this is taking? ___YES ___NO

Are these questions getting on your nerves? ___YES ___NO

If so, why the heck are you still answering them? ___YES ___NO

If we'd just leave you alone, would you be a lot happier? ___YES ___NO

*If you answered "yes" to more than four of these questions, there's a chair for you in the balcony with Statler and Waldorf. If not, there's hope for you. Read on.

## Connecting with Your Inner Tadpole

So why would you want to get back in touch with your inner tadpole? There are three simple reasons:

1. You want to make the most of every day.
2. You want to have someone to talk to when no one else is around.
3. You want to have someone to talk to after you get picked up for walking around talking to yourself.

Let's start by opening a line of communication with your inner tadpole. This is as easy as having a conversation with a friend. Just say, "Hello, inner tadpole, are you there?" and wait for an answer.

* If you get no answer, wait and ask again.
* If you get voicemail, try texting.
* If, however, you hear a little voice inside respond, *Yeah, what is it?* then congratulations, you've reconnected with your inner tadpole.

## Getting to Know You All Over Again

Any kind of reunion is stressful, but a reunion with a part of yourself can be especially difficult. After all, you've been together all those years, sharing the same body, the same mind, the same styling gel, and even the same toothbrush, yet you've been so far apart. While your outer self has been gallivanting around acting like a big frog in a small pond, your inner tadpole has been swimming all by itself, wondering what went wrong.

With that in mind, it's easy to see why these first moments back together are critical. You need to be friendly and sincere, but don't be afraid to use sweet-talking or outright flattery. Inner tadpoles can be very forgiving, but they need to know you still care.

Here are a few phrases that will help you break the ice with your inner tadpole. (These also work with Miss Piggy.)

> **You look beautiful in this light.**

> **I've missed your smile.**

> **I'll pay for everything.**

> **I'm sorry. I was wrong. You were right about all of it.**

Once you've built a rapport with your inner tadpole, it will be time to move on to more difficult topics. It's all about trust. You and your inner tadpole must learn to trust each other again. So you will need to establish certain ground rules as you move forward together. For instance:

* Who makes decisions about how big a tip to leave?
* What holidays does your inner tadpole get to take?
* How good is the health and dental plan?
* What does the retirement plan look like?

When your outer toad sees questions like that, its first inclination is to say, "Call my lawyer!" Actually, that's an outer toad's first inclination in every situation. But you must resist this urge to seek legal counsel. The relationship between you and your inner tadpole is precious and unique. Bringing in some high-priced, take-no-prisoners negotiator is only going to sour things. Take care of things yourself. And remember, when you're negotiating with yourself, it's a win-win situation. Actually, it's also a lose-lose situation, but try not to bring this up.

With these difficult decisions behind you, it's time to move to the next level of consciousness, that blissful state where you and your inner tadpole live in the moment and happily share every day. You are now ready to achieve that oneness I talked about earlier, the enlightenment that comes only when you . . .

## Embrace Your Inner Tadpole

Get comfortable. Put on those fuzzy slippers. Heck, get crazy and make some hot cocoa. The time has come to open your arms to yourself.

Go ahead, put your arms out. I know it looks foolish, but so do those fuzzy bunny slippers, so who cares? Take a deep breath, then another and another. (Remember to keep inhaling and exhaling or you may pass out.)

Close your eyes. Relax your body. And think wonderful thoughts. Go ahead, think of Christmas, think of snow, think of sleigh bells, here we go! Like a reindeer in the sky! You can fly! You can fly! You can fly!

Oh wait, that's the wrong "think" to think. Come back down here. No, please don't take the second star to the right and on straight till morning, or you'll end up in somebody else's book.

Sorry about that.

Now, where were we? Oh, right, close your eyes. Relax your body. Think wonderful thoughts, then reach outward. Because your inner tadpole has no size or shape (which makes buying clothes tough, but is otherwise pretty neat), you won't feel anything when you wrap your arms around them. But you'll know. You'll be filled with happiness. Now close your eyes, embrace, and squeeze.

Not too hard! After all, your inner tadpole is fragile.

That's it. Just like that. Not too much, not too little. Just right. Gentle. Tranquil. Serene. Perfect.

You're at peace with yourself.

Now open your eyes. Are people staring? So what?! You and your inner tadpole are together again.

Hey, you two are great together. Now don't lose touch!

And if you ever want to do a doubles act, give me a call. I'm always looking for talent.

CHAPTER

11

# LOVE
## According
## to
# Muppets

**I** *believe in love. I think love genuinely makes the world a better place. And, sure, there are all different types of love: the love we feel for our friends, the love we feel for our family members, even the love we feel for the tea at our favorite café. I may not be an expert in dating or marriage, but I consider my life to have been happier because of love.*

# Love, Amphibian Style

It's no secret that Miss Piggy and I have shared a complicated on-again, off-again, big, grand, Hollywood relationship. Everyone likes to talk about it, except for me. I like privacy. Please see Chapter Four. Instead, I decided to turn these pages into a tribute to love in its many forms. Y'see, I think for too long, we've seen those sappy happily-ever-afters and been made to believe that if we don't have passionate, committed, 4K HD widescreen

> **What is Love? Love is the most overwhelming feeling in the world, especially if it's coming from a pig.**

romance, there is something missing in our lives. And I'm here to show you that's simply untrue. Sure, dating and marriage are wonderful for some. Others find that same sense of comfort and belonging with friends or family members or pets. So I'd like to spend this chapter reflecting on the other Muppets and their many interpretations of love. It's certainly more interesting than taking romantic advice from a frog with a track record of being run over by an enraged swine.

## Gonzo and Camilla: Egg-ceptional Romance

Gonzo met Camilla when she and some other hens auditioned for *The Muppet Show*. He took one look and it was love. Gonzo and Camilla understand, support, and love each other. Most important of all, they don't care what the world thinks about their relationship. I think that's a beautiful lesson for all of us: Love who you love and never be ashamed of that. If a daredevil can find lifelong happiness with a chicken, who's to judge.

## Robin and Sweetums: Best Friends Come in Every Size

I remember when Robin and Sweetums first met on the set of *The Frog Prince*. It wasn't an immediate best friendship, but it was memorable. Robin was reading his script, understandably nervous for his first big acting role. Sweetums came out of wardrobe dressed as an ogre and rushed over to Robin (who was immediately scared speechless), bellowing, "Hey! Y'wanna read lines together?!" Robin took a moment to collect himself, realizing Sweetums was not, in fact, going to eat him, and then agreed. They've been the best of friends ever since, not the least bit deterred by their difference in heights.

## Rizzo and Pizza: Far from Cheesy

Rizzo has courted a few rats over the years, but the feelings he has for them pale in comparison to those of his one true love: pizza. And to be honest, it's nice to know where we all stand in Rizzo's ranking of love and friendship. He may think of us all fondly and be willing to help out in a pinch, but only if it does not interfere with his access to food. And while pizza tops the list (he even operates that pizzeria in Walt Disney World!), he is equally affectionate toward all manner of edibles, from fresh-picked apples to Victorian jelly beans and from mile-high spaghetti to expertly curated charcuterie. Come to think of it, there really isn't any type of food for which I haven't seen Rizzo declare his love.

## Lew Zealand and His Boomerang Fish: Sole Mates

You've never seen someone as committed to fish as Lew Zealand. He's no ichthyologist, he's just really dedicated to throwing fish and having them return. It's a variety act. It's a skill. It's a hobby. It's fundamentally who Lew is. Lew loves his fish and has dedicated his life to their aerial stunts. Some loves are difficult to explain but impossible to deny.

## Sam Eagle and America: Heart of a Patriot

I asked to include Sam in this list because I think it's important to note that love isn't always a physical person, or a snack, or a projectile-slash-aquatic-friend. Sometimes love is an ideal. And for Sam Eagle, his love of America runs deep. And I mean deep. Like 86-meters-below-sea-level, Badwater-Basin deep. (Badwater Basin is the lowest point in North America. I was going for a geographical simile here.) Like America, Sam isn't always perfect. But they both strive to be the best versions of themselves. Although Sam's love of America and decency and American decency may get a little overzealous at times, it makes him happy. And love should make us happy, right?

## Dr. Bunsen Honeydew and Beaker: Data Inconclusive

Ever the scientist, Dr. Bunsen tried to explain why he and Beaker should not be included in this chapter, citing that while there are chemical reactions that trigger cranial receptors, it is impossible for science to predict or explain love. But I think they're a perfect example of love because of the trust and dedication they have for each other and the deep commitment they share for the advancement of science. If you can share your career with someone, who's to say that isn't professional love?

## Sgt. Floyd Pepper and Animal: Keep on Keeping On

Floyd and Animal share a special bond that goes all the way

back to when Animal was a baby. Not much is known about Animal—where he came from, or what species he is, or where he goes at night—but we do know that Animal is fiercely loyal to those he loves. And I think that's a quality he learned growing up on the road with Floyd. (Well, that and an appreciation for loud music.) Floyd isn't quite a father figure for Animal, but he's certainly more than a friend. He's one of those rare and special people who become found family, the kinds you would protect at all costs. And if that isn't love, I don't know what is.

# What Is This Thing Called Love?

No one truly understands love. Edison can invent the lightbulb, NASA can send a man to the moon, and Einstein can come up with theories about his relatives, but nobody has ever figured out why one person loves another. As Dr. Bunsen said, if there's a formula for romantic success, it has yet to be discovered. Maybe that's why we all love to love. It's always surprising. It's sometimes annoying. But it is never dull. It can lift you up with joy or send you down into the depths of despair, all in the stretch of a minute and a half.

So don't sweat finding that big Hollywood romance. Maybe when you least expect it, you'll bump into that special someone who puts a twinkle in your eye. I'm glad that Piggy is in my life. Really. I mean it. Oh sure, she and I have different opinions about the nature of our relationship, but we care deeply for each other. And I wouldn't have it any other way. She can be a bit much sometimes, and way too much a lot of the time, but she really wants to be loved. (Okay, so she also wants to be reimbursed, rewarded, and celebrated, but that's just a matter of degree.) Beneath it all, Piggy is just like the rest of us—searching for acceptance and appreciation in a world that can be tough at times.

I think that's what we're all looking for. And whether it's a romantic partner, a friend, a sibling, a pet, a hobby, a career, an ideal, or any other kind of love that's true to you, I hope that it brings you that sense of acceptance and appreciation. Wherever you are in your journey, remember to celebrate all the different types of love in your life. Some are big and some are small. But all of those loves matter. Soak up the acceptance and appreciation and try to pass some along, too. That's what love is all about. We only get so many days on this earth, so to spend that time loving and being loved is a life well-lived.

# CHAPTER

## 12

# Better with Friends

**I**f there's anything I hope you learned from the last chapter, it's that I love my friends. I guess that's pretty obvious. After all, I spend almost every moment with Fozzie, Gonzo, Animal, Miss Piggy, and the rest of The Muppets. We live together, eat together, vacation together, and all seem to want to get into the bathroom at exactly the same time. We're close. Very close. Very, very, very close. And I wouldn't have it any other way. (Except maybe to add on a couple of extra bathrooms.) My friends are my life. Oh sure, I love being a celebrity, but that wouldn't mean anything if I couldn't share those moments with friends.

## The Power of Friendship

If you have good friends like I do, you know exactly what I mean. Friends are the whipped topping on the ice-cream sundae of life, with a few nuts thrown in for good measure.

Of course, not all of us have these kinds of strong friendships. Some of us are shy. Some of us don't yet know how to break the ice. Some of us are a tad strange. No problem! I'm here to show you how to make new friends and how to build lasting relationships with everyone you meet.

C'mon all you shy, strange, novice icebreakers. Step inside and stick close to the frog. It's time to mingle!

## Friendship: A 14-Step Program

Making friends is easy once you know the rules.

"There are rules?!" you gasp.

Yup, there are rules—fourteen rules, to be exact—to making and keeping friends. I've been making acquaintances for years, so I should know. Early on I didn't put much thought into making friends. How difficult could it be?

Very difficult, it turns out. A good friendship needs care and attention. It is your shelter and your comfort—a place to laugh, cry, sing, dance, and borrow money when times are tight. And more than all of that, a friend is someone who is always there for you, who believes in you no matter what happens, and who you believe in, too.

If you want that kind of friendship, the kind that lasts a lifetime and stands up to wear and tear, hard times, small slights, and stress fractures of all sorts, then you have to work for it. But don't get discouraged. It's easy, once you know the fourteen rules of friendship.

## 1.
### Be Happy with Who You Are.

What's that, you say—the first rule is about me? Absolutely. If you want others to like you, first you have to like yourself. And I mean really, genuinely like the person that you are and believe in what you have to offer to the world. Look at yourself in the mirror and say, "Hey, you look like a friendly sort! Happy to meet you." This is not only good for your self-esteem, it's great practice for meeting others. But remember, don't try to shake hands with your reflection. (Broken mirrors aren't just bad luck; you can get a nasty cut, too.) Once you like you, it's time to move on to . . .

## 2.
### Begin Every Interaction in a Friendly Manner.

If you want to make friends, start by being friendly. That sounds logical. Yet you'd be surprised by how many people make a bad first impression. Take Statler and Waldorf, who tend to greet people with a one-two punch of insults.

**We hear that you're one of a kind.**

**And that's one too many! Do-ho-ho-ho-ho!**

Instead, follow the lead of Fozzie Bear, whose trademark "Hiya! Hiya!" not only announces the arrival of a very friendly bear, but also serves to warn all within earshot that jokes are coming, so stand back. As for myself, I use the traditional amphibian greeting, Hi-ho! Please feel free to borrow it, or come up with your own personalized friendly greeting.

## 3.

### Be Genuinely Interested in Others.

The secret here is to listen to what others are saying. Sometimes when we first meet a new person, we're so concerned about what we're going to say next that we pay absolutely no attention to what the other person is speaking about. If you listen, chances are you'll discover that this person is saying something fascinating or useful or at least mildly distracting. There are exceptions to this rule. For instance, at parties Dr. Bunsen Honeydew and Beaker have been known to do a solid hour and a half of quantum physics jokes. These are the social equivalent of a black hole, sucking in all light, air, and any remaining microparticles of interest (What do you get when you take a room full of lumberjacks and mathematicians to see clog dancing? Logger-Rhythm dancing). And yet, even under these extreme conditions, it is possible to find something interesting about the speakers. For as I stood there, trying to grapple with that joke . . . Oh, wait, I get it: logarithm dancing. Yeesh!

# 4.
## Be a Great Listener.

I've never had a problem with this one, at least not since I met Miss Piggy. Keeping up a conversation with her mostly involves listening. This is a way to show the person that you care about what she has to say and find her utterly fascinating. It's also a great way to let the other person do all the heavy conversational lifting. You don't have to worry about arriving at a party with a stash of intriguing anecdotes and clever quips, because you're just going to stand there with a smile on your face, nodding and trying desperately to keep your eyes open. Of course, there is always the danger that you will meet people who have the same idea as you. They came here planning to smile and nod. So one tip I picked up to avoid potentially awkward gaps in the conversation: Ask them questions about what they're saying. Questions show that you're paying attention and you're interested, and, as long as you don't turn the conversation into a full-fledged interview, are a great way to connect with new people.

# 5.
## Show Respect to Everyone.

It doesn't matter who a person is, what they/she/he look like, or what they do for a living. What matters is that they/she/he are another person and therefore deserve your respect. I think it's awful when someone is disrespectful just because they think the other person doesn't deserve to be treated decently. I can't tell you how many times I've been overlooked just because I'm two feet

tall. No one likes to be looked down on, which is why I always bring a stack of phone books to stand on wherever I go. It's also why I go out of my way to show respect to each and every person I meet. And what's the best way to show respect? Well, Miss Piggy believes that giving money and jewels is the best way. But I believe that just being polite is enough. Saying "thank you" and "it's an honor to meet you" goes a long way toward making people feel respected.

## 6.
## Expect the Best from Others.

Statler and Waldorf have a saying: "Expect the worst . . . and never be disappointed." This is the exact opposite of Rule #6. If you are certain that others will treat you poorly or take advantage of you, you've already lost them as possible friends. You should enter every relationship expecting the best from your new acquaintance. People will want to live up to your expectations; they'll actually rise to the occasion! And if they come to you with the same attitude, chances are that you'll do your best to rise to meet their expectations. But remember, no one is perfect, so if someone slips and isn't all that you expected them to be, give that person the benefit of the doubt. (Of course, if they slip a lot, you may want to reconsider, which is why I never let Pepé help count money, but still consider him a friend.)

## 7.
## Appeal to Others' Higher Motives.

Sometimes it seems as if all others in the world are looking out only for themselves. If you can't do something for them, they don't want to have anything to do with you. You get this attitude all the time: "What's in it for me?" Hearing this can convince you that the only way to interest other people is to appeal to their baser instincts. That might be true with some people, but I've discovered that most of us believe in doing the right thing and helping others. Kindness. Compassion. Charity. Decency. Personal hygiene. These and other such higher ideals speak to our best selves. Try appealing to this best side of others and you just might be surprised at how well other folks respond. It has worked for me; just look at my friends. They're the kindest, most compassionate, most charitable, most decent, and, with the possible exception of Rizzo, most personally hygienic group you'd ever want to meet.

## 8.

## Be Open to New Things.

I've always tried to be as open as possible to new people, new things, and new, well, whatevers. As a result, I find myself constantly surrounded by new people, new things, and most especially new whatevers. You might even say that The Muppets define the concept of openness. Where else will you find such an incredibly diverse and multicultural gathering of individuals? And unlike those talk shows, we rarely throw chairs or have to be wrestled to the ground by burly security guards. Oh sure, there are times when our happy little group experiences some tension, but for the most part we accept and even embrace each other's differences. As a result we have created a cross-generational, cross-species network of friendships that will last forever. Try being open to the "new" in your life, and you may soon find yourself in the warm embrace of a similar group of friends. (Don't say you haven't been warned!)

## Have a Sense of Humor.

Ask most people what they look for in a friend and the first quality they'll mention is "a sense of humor." (Piggy is the exception here. Although it is true that she wants friends with a sense of humor, this is not the first quality she seeks. It's number seven on the list of demands that include financial support, social media followers, and unlimited beach access in Malibu.) For most of us, finding friends with a good sense of humor is the best of all possible worlds. We all want to laugh, and to be with friends who can share our laughter. When you break into a chuckle, chortle, giggle, or guffaw, you want the world to chuck, chort, gig, and guff right along with you. It lifts the heart; it replenishes the soul. But to attract people with a sense of humor, you have to have a sense of humor, too. In my experience I've found that there are four types, or "senses," of humor:

**Natural-Born Sense of Humor.** Most of us see the funny side of things.
**Professional Sense of Humor.** Fozzie has a refined and polished comedian's sense of humor, for which he pays joke writer Gags Beasley a handsome sum.
**Specialized Sense of Humor.** Some folks find only certain things funny. For instance, Statler and Waldorf will laugh only if the joke is on you.
**No Sense of Humor.** Sam Eagle does not find this (or anything else) amusing in the least.

Choose the sense of humor that's closest to yours. When you meet someone with a similar outlook on life, you'll have found a friend who "gets" it.

# 10.
## Be Honest and Be Kind.

"Honesty is the best policy," wrote Ben Franklin, who lived more than two hundred years ago and therefore didn't have to put his policy to the test in an age of smartphones and influencers. But I do. And despite having suffered the slings and arrows of this century, I must agree with Ben. It is always best to be honest. Friendship is about sharing everything with another person. If you can't share the bad news as well as the good, it's not much of a friendship. That's not to say that anyone enjoys getting or giving bad news. But sometimes it's necessary to be honest even when someone's feelings might get hurt.

That's where the second part comes in: Never use honesty as an excuse to be unkind or hurtful. Sometimes I have to tell Fozzie that his joke didn't land. And when I do, I try to be as kind as possible. I think that's what being a good friend is all about.

# 11.
## Avoid Arguments.

I don't like to argue. I'm a go-along-to-get-along kind of frog—a trait I get from growing up around hungry alligators, I guess. If you want a friendship that really works, do your best to avoid arguing. Here's what I do: I try to see all sides of an issue, let people voice their opinions, then try to help folks reach a consensus through reasoned debate and civilized discourse. Only after this thoughtful process inevitably degenerates into a full-scale, no-holds-barred melee do I resort to that time-honored method of conflict resolution: waving my spindly arms in the air and yelling in a high-pitched voice until I run out of air and pass out. Dignified it's not, but it sure is effective. While the arguing people are trying to revive me, they usually end up resolving their differences before I come to . . . and just in time for me to treat everyone to lunch. It's costly, but it sure beats arguing.

## 12.
### Admit Mistakes.

Owning up to mistakes is the best way to save a floundering friendship. Be forthcoming. Admit you did something wrong. Ask for forgiveness. It will make your friendships last. I'm very good at admitting mistakes. Thanks to Miss Piggy, I've had a lot of practice.

## 13.
### Be Quick to Forgive.

This is the flip side of admitting mistakes. When friends admit a mistake to you, don't be angry or hold a grudge. Let them know that (a) you appreciate their honesty and (b) whatever they did is forgotten and forgiven forever. Wouldn't you want them to treat you the same way? I know I would.

## 14.
### Give Your Time and Your Talents When You Can.

When you can give your time and your talents to others without expecting anything in return, your friends appreciate it. (I've found that a secret to this tip is the "when you can"—because part of being a good friend is looking out for yourself, too. So give your time and your talents when you're in a healthy head space to do so, and find friends who understand the importance of that balance.) Oh, and don't think that you don't have talents to share! Everyone does, whether it's sharing a story, mending a sock, building a subatomic particle generator (thanks, Dr. Honeydew!), or telling a joke. That last talent is one of the big reasons why Fozzie and I are such good friends. No matter what else he's doing, Fozzie is always ready to share a joke with me. Oh sure, it's probably a joke I've heard before. Many times. But he gives it selflessly, and I appreciate the gesture even though I still don't get the punch line.

Well, there you have it. Follow the fourteen rules of friendship and before you know it you'll have friends just like mine. And I mean that as a good thing.

I couldn't be this cool without all of my pals!

# CHAPTER

# 13

# Dealing
## with
## Fame & Good
## FORTUNE

**W**ho out there doesn't want to rub elbows with influential people, the kind who can change the course of mighty nations, break world records, and be charismatic on late-night talk shows? But as I've gone through life, I've discovered something amazing about these so-called influential people: They really are just like you and me. Y'see, influential people are regular folks who have talent, luck, good fortune, and gumption to achieve more clout, higher visibility, and better seats at Lakers games. If you want to meet them—and network with them, as they say in the biz—you just need to follow the aforementioned rules for building friendships. And what if you, too, should achieve that level of fame? Well, it may sound like a great thing from afar, but there's a lot more to it than you might imagine. Read on.

# Being True to Yourself

My life has never been about getting rich and being famous, signed contracts notwithstanding. To me, wealth and fame are nice extras that sometimes come with doing what you love and can be shared with the people you care about. What really matters is making people happy, making yourself and your friends happy, and making the world a better place to live in.

Some folks take being rich and famous very seriously. I guess I can understand why. Having money is handy. You can buy stuff for friends, family, and yourself, plus you can use the money to help others. As for fame, it has some advantages, too. For instance, you get recognized when you go places, and you get to meet other famous people you've never met before and pretend that you're close personal friends who've known each other for years.

How has being rich and famous changed me? Not too much, I'd say. Personally, I'm not big on buying stuff. Oh sure, I enjoy getting new strings for my banjo or having my lily pad reupholstered with new moss, but otherwise I'm not much of a consumer. Because I rarely wear clothes or shoes, my wardrobe needs are minimal. And when I travel, I actually prefer to fly cargo. There's more legroom and more fresh air, and for in-flight entertainment we go through other people's luggage. You should try it sometime.

As for being famous, I can see only one real benefit: I get to meet famous people. I'm the first to admit that it's a thrill to meet someone whose work I've admired over the years. When I find myself face-to-face with movie stars, I am exactly like any other fan . . . only shorter. I want to say something memorable and witty, but I usually end up ribbeting incoherently. Fortunately, most famous people assume I'm saying something in my native language and simply ribbet in response.

Because of my own experiences as a fan, I always do my best to make my fans feel comfortable when we meet. I can't tell you how many times people have come up to me at a restaurant and been too nervous to speak. They stand there slack-jawed, not knowing how to begin. I always try to put them at ease, make them feel welcome, and—if they happen to be our waiter—give them our dinner order. Once folks realize that I'm just like any other talking frog, they loosen up, and we always have a great conversation. Talking to people from all over the world and learning that something I've done has made them laugh is a truly magical experience.

In the first edition of this book, Miss Piggy was not shy with her recommendations and thoughts around this chapter. So for this edition, I thought I'd turn over the reins to the one and only Miss Piggy for her secrets to success. Piggy, take it away!

# Kissy kissy! 'Tis moi! Miss Piggy!

I'm guest hosting, as it were, in my dearest Kermie's book. The sweet boy is handsome, talented, and wise about the world. But let's be honest here. You don't really want advice about getting ahead in life from a frog. You want battle-tested strategies and in-your-face tactics from a world-class diva. And that, my dear reader, is *moi*! So let's take a look at Moi's Secrets for Success, the only guide you'll ever need for getting to the top and staying there.

## Miss Piggy's Secrets for Success

**DEFINE YOUR OWN SUCCESS.** We all have a different idea of what success means to us. For *moi*, it includes acclaim, admiration, adulation, and plenty of freebies. Your goals may be less grand—and probably should be because you aren't *moi* to begin with, so why invite disappointment? But it is critical that you know what success means to you from the start; otherwise, when you get there, *vous* will be lost, kind of like this sentence, which *moi* can't figure out how to end so I'm just going to stop now.

**TREAT OTHERS AS YOU WANT TO BE TREATED.** This is sometimes known as the golden rule, although *moi* cannot imagine why because there is no mention of gold or any other precious metals anywhere in it. Nonetheless I have discovered that it is always in your best interest to be kind and generous with those around you, no matter who they are. For instance, when handing your keys to that red-jacketed person who will park your car, say "Good evening" and "Thank you" rather than "Don't dent the fenders, chowderhead!" Otherwise, you may never, ever see your car again. Don't ask how I know this; I just do.

**DON'T WORRY ABOUT YOUR WEALTH.** Money means nothing to me. I don't think about it, and I don't worry about it. Just ask someone who has spent time with *moi*. I almost never carry money. After all, if you're going to hang out with rich people, why not let them pay?

**DON'T WORRY ABOUT YOUR SIZE.** Let *moi* start by saying that I'm not one of those people who is obsessed with my body shape. The world is shaped by people brave enough to be themselves and make their mark. So why should you change to fit someone else's vision of *vous*? Be yourself, embrace what makes you unique, and don't listen to what the media has to say about ideal weights or figures. Some famous people starve themselves to fit into a certain dress. But every outfit eventually goes out of fashion, so you'll have wasted all that time starving and turned down all those desserts for nothing. I think as long as *moi* is happy and healthy, my size is irrelevant.

**BE GENEROUS OF SPIRIT.** No matter where you are on the ladder of success, share your joyous spirit with others. It costs nothing to bubble with ebullience, overflow with good cheer, and otherwise be the life of the party. When you share such happiness, you are giving something that is not only priceless, it doesn't cost you a cent. Naturally, as you rise ever higher on the ladder of success, you should continue to share your joy, preferably wrapped in a lovely jewelry box tied with a bow—and preferably shared with me.

**BE HUMBLE.** When one is heaped with praise and buried in accolades, it can be difficult to remain modest and unassuming. As the tributes wash across your doorstep, it is almost impossible to fight the urge to be arrogant and egotistical. Believe it or not, *moi* has had to fight this battle time and time again.

And though I have always remained timid and self-effacing, it hasn't been easy. There is always temptation to blow one's own horn, so to speak. Resist this temptation. Make your publicist blow your horn. There's no sense making a spectacle of yourself when someone else is getting paid to do it for *vous*.

**BE REAL.** When you achieve success, whether it be wealth or fame, or merely notoriety and temporary use of someone else's cash, it's a very good thing if no one knows who you are. Nonetheless, it's best to figure out who you are and remain true to your character no matter what. Many people on the road to success try to change themselves. They constantly alter their personality, desperately attempting to be what they think the world wants them to be. This is silly. First, there are far too many people in the world to please everyone. Second, you won't meet most of these people in person, so why bother trying? And third, if you're going to please anyone, make it *moi*.

**KNOW YOUR CORE VALUES.** What are core values? Beats me, but everyone seems to be talking about them, so I'm guessing they must be important. Now, from what I can gather, these core values are the ones that mean the most to you. These are the things in your life that you would not trade or change no matter what. So, for instance, *moi*'s core values are chocolate, fashion, my dog Foo-Foo, and of course my adoring fans. If I am true to these values, everything else will take care of itself. If I am untrue to these values, I'll get cranky and probably end up throwing a hissy fit, at least until somebody finds some more chocolate. So I am never untrue to my core values. I suggest you seek your own core values. Consider what is most important in life to you and be true to these things.

**THINK TWICE BEFORE POSTING.** Believe me when I say, the Internet is forever. I don't actually know how it works, but I believe it has something to do with lots of letters and numbers flying through the air and reassembling themselves as selfies. Bunsen tried to explain it once, but I wasn't paying attention. Regardless, in this digital age, one piece of advice *moi* must impart is the importance of uploading with care. Post too often and your fans get bored. Post too rarely and your followers forget you exist. Post the wrong photo, and even after you delete the post, it will live on in social media screenshots and Internet tabloids for all time. Trust me. It's a jungle out there.

**WHATEVER YOU HAVE, GIVE IT AWAY.** Lest you think I'm about to hand over my jewels, designer wardrobe, and personal fortune, allow *moi* to straighten *vous* out. Those valuable "things" are fine for what they are, but it would be too easy for *moi* to simply give away "things." When I say to give away whatever you have, I am talking about giving away the very essence of success. And that's my advice—free of charge. If that's not selfless, I don't know what is. And let me remind you that this isn't even *moi's* book. It's Kermie's, so *moi* is not getting a dime in return for sharing all this marvelous advice. Yes, dear friends, these secrets for success are *moi's* gift to you, a way of sharing everything I have without actually having to give up anything.

Oh, by the way, this is not the complete list of Moi's Secrets for Success. It's what we in the business of showbiz call a teaser or trailer. If you want the complete list, including detailed plans for starting your own at-home success-advice business, then you'll just have to fork over some cash to buy my online course, Moi-ster Class . . . just as soon as I hire some overachieving intern to film and edit it for me.

XOXO,

*Miss Piggy*
XX

# How to Be Famous...
# Even When You Don't Want to Be

I have to admit that I wasn't fully prepared for being "famous." When you're short and green and live in a swamp with several thousand short, green brothers, sisters, and cousins, as well as fellow frogs, toads, and other assorted amphibians, being overlooked is par for the course. And that's just fine with me. I do what I do to make folks happy, not to sparkle.

But fame happens. And these days, with viral videos, social media influencers, and nonstop push notifications, it seems to happen to just about everyone, everywhere, all the time. You don't have to sign a rich-and-famous contract anymore; it's more like fame puts out a contract on you. One moment you're filming a movie about your evil döppelganger taking your place on a European tour, and the next minute you're a viral meme.

That's great! It can be fun to be famous . . . at first. But pretty soon, it gets a bit overwhelming.

Suddenly, it seems as if someone is always in your face—going through your trash, posting about what you had for breakfast, and live streaming your every move. It can be annoying. It can be maddening. And if you're not ready for it, it can make you do what I do—throw your hands up in the air, wave your arms wildly, and run rapidly from the room yelling "Yaaaaaaaaaghhhh!" (That video of me throwing my hands up in the air, waving my arms wildly, and running rapidly from the room yelling "Yaaaaaaaaaghhhh!" also went viral, leading to even more attention. Sheesh!)

Fame used to be for the few—those hearty souls in Hollywood who spent a lifetime reaching for the golden statue and along the way became household names. But today, fame is for everyone. And not everyone is prepared. Well, there are two ways to handle fame. You can deal with it gracefully, doing your best to maintain your privacy, your dignity, and your calm. Or you can embrace fame, wrap yourself around it, hug, hold, cuddle, and crush it . . . and never, ever let it go.

I am a proponent of the former method. I enjoy being recognized, even if I am sometimes mistaken for one of the other short, green Hollywood stars. I enjoy signing autographs and making people smile. It feels great! But I also need my alone time—a chance to sit on a lily pad and ponder the mysteries of the universe and the possibilities of snagging that dragonfly for dinner. I like fame, but I still try to keep it at arm's length.

Not surprisingly, Miss Piggy takes the exact opposite approach, and she is mistress of her domain. She doesn't merely deal with fame—she is a one-woman fame factory, churning out gossip, campaigning for awards, fueling trending topics, and doing whatever else will get her attention. It seems that I can't pick up a magazine, read a newspaper, turn on a television, or

go online without seeing Miss Piggy's face. She's everywhere!

So, how will you handle fame: the Kermit approach or the Miss Piggy approach?

To make your choice easier, here are three common celebrity situations—and a look at how Miss Piggy handles them and how I handle them. Look them over, then decide which approach works best for you. But be forewarned: If you decide to go the Miss Piggy route, don't ever try to go headline-to-headline with her. Trust me.

## Celebrity Scenario #1: Paparazzi Ambush

You're about to enter a restaurant, when from out of nowhere dozens . . . no, make that hundreds of paparazzi descend upon you, snapping pictures, shouting, and trying to get you so riled up that you'll do something outrageous for a great picture.

**THE KERMIT APPROACH:** I stop and smile. I let all the paparazzi get as many pictures as they want, and then I go in and enjoy my dinner. Admittedly, this can take time. I've had more than a few restaurants close while I was accommodating the press. But if it goes on long enough, I send for takeout and eat right there with the paparazzi. By the way, they have very healthy appetites, so order extra.

**THE MISS PIGGY APPROACH:** Act surprised! Shocked! Strike a series of "oh my!" poses. Pause briefly for a wardrobe change, then repeat the same surprise-shock-oh my! reaction. After you've done this with three or four different fashion ensembles, you can either enter the restaurant to enjoy your dinner or you can ask "What? No helicopters?!" thereby allowing you to go through the whole routine again, but this time with very impressive aerial coverage.

# Celebrity Scenario #2: The Famous Feud

Somehow a rumor got out that you and some other famous person are feuding. It can be about anything (e.g., star billing, who gets the biggest trailer, etc.), but it's usually about absolutely nothing. In fact, it's usually totally made up. But with celebrities (as with politicians), truth is secondary. You have to deal with it. What do you do?

**THE KERMIT APPROACH:** Make peace. First, figure out whom you're supposed to be mad at and arrange for the two of you to meet with the press. Smile. Shake hands. Express confusion about how this "feud" rumor ever got started and make it clear that you two would love to work together and are longtime pals.

**THE MISS PIGGY APPROACH:** Attack! Attack! Attack! The best offense is not a good defense, it's to be as offensive as possible. Even if there is no truth to this feud rumor, and even if you have no idea who you're supposedly feuding with, go after them with fresh rumors and fake tears. Use words like "scurrilous," "defamatory," and "actionable"! Have no idea what these words mean? Not a problem. If you repeat them often enough, they'll not only make it into print, you may even learn how to pronounce them correctly.

# Celebrity Scenario #3: The Scandal du Jour

You may be a good person with impeccable habits who actually oozes kindness from your pores. (I have an uncle in the swamp who can do that.) And yet, once fame comes into your life, you find yourself in the middle of various scandals. You didn't do anything wrong! But somehow they've got you mixed up with deadbeats, malcontents, wasters, and ne'er-do-wells of every stripe. It doesn't really matter what the scandal is; you've been linked to it, and if you don't do something quickly, you'll be on the wrong side of public opinion.

**THE KERMIT APPROACH:** Complete honesty. If there's even a shred of truth to the scandal, admit it and apologize. Vow to make sure that something like this will never happen again. (This can be difficult, especially when you're not sure what happened, but give it a try anyhow.) And if there's no truth to the scandal, then say that. Let the world know that you have been falsely defamed and that you will not rest until the false defamer admits they were wrong. Of course, the false defamer almost never admits they were wrong, but quickly gets bored that you're not playing the game and moves on to the next scandal. And that's good enough for me.

**THE MISS PIGGY APPROACH:** How dare they insinuate that you are involved in scandalous behavior! You weren't there! You've never been there! You might go there if someone has directions, but let's worry about that later. If you actually have no connection to the scandal, this might work. If you are, indeed, a party to the scandal . . . well, it won't get you out of a jam, but it will keep the coverage roaring for weeks on end. And really, how bad can a scandal be if you can get several weeks of coverage out of it, *n'est ce pas*?!

Well, there you have it, a frog's-and-pig's-eye view of fame and how to deal with it. Only you can decide what suits your needs. But if there's one thing I hope you remember, it's to never lose sight of the real you. Don't let fame and fortune change you, because you're great just as you are. I can't wait to ask you for your autograph!

CHAPTER

14

# The Amphibious Art of Relaxation

**T**aking it easy is something that a lot of people simply forget to do. They get so caught up in their day-to-day struggle to make a living and get ahead that they don't enjoy themselves. They don't stop to smell the roses, sit back to watch the sunset, or, my personal favorite, pause to pluck a banjo by the bayou.

Hi-ho? Piggy? Anybody here?!

## Tips for Taking It Easy

All work and no play can make for a dull life. Just ask Sam Eagle. Day and night, he thinks about nothing but his job. For Sam, there is no separation between work and play. Relaxation makes him tense, so he avoids it. And if he's perfectly happy never being perfectly happy, good for Sam!

The flip side of this approach is epitomized by Rizzo the Rat, known everywhere as a veritable "conno-sewer" of relaxation. For Rizzo, all play and no work is the only way to go. If something involves heavy lifting, light lifting, or even lifting a finger, Rizzo doesn't want any part of it. I'm impressed by Rizzo's dedication to his craft. I've never seen anyone work so hard at not working.

But most of us aren't like Sam Eagle or Rizzo the Rat. We work hard, but we also want to enjoy our lives. And yet, when it comes to relaxation, many of us don't know where to begin. How does one relax? How do you develop a hobby that you'll actually enjoy and want to do? What kind of diversion is right for you and your free time?

By this point you may be wondering why it's so important to find something to do with your free time. The answer is really quite simple: If you don't find something fun to do with your free time, someone else will find something to do with you and your free time. It could involve extra hours at work, mowing the lawn, or volunteering at high-stress bake sales at schools that neither you nor your loved ones attend.

And take it from me: It probably won't be fun. So I'm here to help you on your quest for relaxation by taking all the hard work out of not working. Although I haven't covered all the possibilities, I think most of you will find something that sounds like fun, or at least sounds better than doing yard work or baking six dozen gluten-free brownies.

Let's get lazy, shall we?

## Relaxing Kermit-Style

**GOLF.** There is nothing more exhilarating than spending an afternoon chasing a very small white ball around a very large, tree-lined, sand-trap-strewn obstacle course, then trying to coax that ball into a tiny hole with a flag in it. Eighteen times. Exhilarating, yes; relaxing, not for this frog.

Don't get me wrong; golf can be a great game. But it's just not for me. I think the biggest problem I have is the greens. No, it's not that my putting is poor; it's that I'm the same color as the greens, and the fairways for that matter. And believe me, fellow golfers don't yell "fore!" when they can't see you. My other big problem has to do with my eyes. It's not the usual complaint about not being able to see all the way to the hole or not being able to keep my eye on the ball. No, the problem is that my eyes look like the ball. When you're out on the fairway, nothing is more distracting than having your fellow golfer swing a nine iron at your noggin,

*Ahhh, I know how to relax. Join me!*

especially when he ends up slicing you into the rough.

There are some things I do like about golfing. I fit in the golf bag, which means my caddy can carry me around the course. This isn't half bad, as long as I don't mind wearing a club cover on my head every time the caddy gets distracted. I also enjoy a part of the game that other golfers hate: the water hazard. Not only is this a chance for me to take a quick dip in the middle of a long, hot day, but I usually run into some relatives there, or at least a toad or a turtle from the old neighborhood.

**FISHING.** Speaking of water, here's a sport that's more my speed. What could be better than sitting in the middle of a lake? Heck, I come from a long line of lake sitters. Whether you're in a boat or standing midstream in hip waders, there's nothing more relaxing than a day spent fishing in the great outdoors.

The only part of fishing I don't understand—and don't do myself—is the actual fishing part. First of all, why would anyone want to put a worm on a hook? I find that the worms are fresher and tastier served straight from the mud. And what's the point of putting the hook into the water and trying to pull a fish into your boat? If you want to visit with a fish, call ahead. Or just drop in. Fish love company. But they don't like leaving home. A fish out of water may be a good Hollywood movie plot, but when real fish are out of their element, their

Fishing can be relaxing . . . sometimes!

conversation tends to *flounder*. (Flounder joke courtesy of Fozzie Bear.)

I'll take fly-fishing any day! Heck, who needs fish? Just give me the flies.

**GARDENING.** Slowing things even more to the refreshingly sedate, I hereby sing the praises of raising greens. Whether you want to plant a plethora of rainbow-hued flowers or a variety of farm-fresh vegetables, you are in for a wonderful time. Oh sure, there'll be a lot of digging, weeding, watering, cultivating, weeding, pruning, trimming, tying, weeding, and . . . Hold on, I need to get some lemonade.

Okay, a garden may be a lot of work. In fact, it's the most work you'll ever do when you're not working. But it's well worth it. There's nothing tastier than homegrown veggies—and the insects they attract. And there's nothing more spectacular than a bouquet of flowers you grew with your very own green thumb. So get out there and garden, but take it from me: If the rest of you is as green as your thumb, beware of errant weed whackers.

**COOKING.** I have a large collection of cookbooks, which I use all the time. Not for the recipes, but to stand on so I can reach the counter. When it comes to the culinary arts, I believe in experimenting with ingredients. I throw in a little of this, a little of that, and a whole bunch of the other thing, then call out for pizza. My creations may not be very edible, but I just love being in the kitchen.

To improve my cooking skills, I've started taking one of the Swedish Chef's Gøød Køøking classes. The chef is difficult to understand, and his concepts are tough to digest, but after only one class I've already learned how to make a mess. It can only get better from here. I hope.

**COLLECTING.** Some folks collect coins and stamps; others collect lunch boxes or first-edition books. The fact is, you can collect almost anything these days.

Let your imagination run wild. We sure do. For instance, Dr. Bunsen Honeydew collects vintage lab equipment, which he then tests on Beaker. Dr. Teeth, Floyd, Animal, Lips, Janice, and Zoot collect classic Electric Mayhem rock-concert posters—not for their artistic value, but in their continuing effort to figure out where the heck they've been on this long, strange trip of theirs. Miss Piggy collects shoes and designer clothes, which she then bills back to me. Fozzie, of course, collects and tells old jokes. And Gonzo collects nicks, abrasions, and contusions. As for me, I used to collect butterflies, until one night when I got real hungry.

Now I collect rainbows. Yup, whenever I see a rainbow, I get out my camera and take a picture. And if I don't have a camera, I just make a wish.

**BOOK CLUBS.** I love to read. It's a chance to escape from everyone and journey off into a world of fantasy and imagination. It's so solitary and relaxing.

That is why I decided to join a book club and share my passion for the written word with others. I pictured us engaged in profound dialogues, with flights of didactic reasoning sure to fill us with wonder as we tried to figure out what "didactic" meant.

That's the book club I imagined I was joining; it's not the book club I joined. Our feisty little gathering—Miss Piggy, Fozzie Bear, Beaker, Rizzo, and myself—spends most of our time arguing over what book to read. Piggy wants to read the blogs, Fozzie wants joke books, no one is sure what Beaker wants, and Rizzo just wants to eat. As for me, I end up sitting off in the corner reading by myself. Like I said, reading is solitary and relaxing.

**SPECTATOR SPORTS.** Go to a game—baseball, basketball, football, soccer. Sure, you aren't playing, but there's something about being at the game that makes for an especially relaxing time. You shout, you scream, you do the wave, and you spill food all over your friends and family. Heck, it's just like dinnertime!

I love basketball, but in Hollywood no one goes to actually watch the game. They go to see who's sitting where. This explains the serious A-list squabbles over who gets the best courtside seats.

All that doesn't matter to me. I just like to watch great athletes at work. Not many players in the major leagues are frogs, which is a shame. Here's hoping more amphibians are drafted in the upcoming seasons.

*My short stint as a goalie.*

**BINGE-WATCHING.** Streaming a show isn't exactly the world's most exciting leisure-time activity. But it sure is convenient. And I'm good at it, too. There's something comforting about closing the curtains, ordering delivery, and curling up to watch an entire series over the course

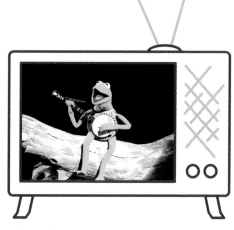

of one weekend. I don't want to suggest that television should be your only hobby. But viewed in moderation and with an eye toward programs that are informative and elevating (or that feature The Muppets), it's kinda nice to enjoy TV as a hobby sometimes. Besides, we Muppets need the gig.

**MENTORING.** To me, this is the very best way to spend your free time. Find a youngster who needs guidance, and be that youngster's role model.

In my life that youngster is my nephew Robin. We do lots of stuff together, but our all-time favorite activity is the Frog Scouts. Along with his Scout troop, we go camping, fishing, hiking, climbing, and even spelunking. (We're not all that big on caves; we just really like to say "spelunking.") As a former Scout myself, I serve as the Scout leader, helping Robin and his friends earn merit badges in such varied areas as first aid, public speaking, environmental awareness, and helping old ladies cross the street without getting squooshed ourselves. You don't have to be a frog or a Scout to be a mentor. And I'm not the only one who understands the importance of mentoring. In fact, almost all of The Muppets are involved in sharing what they know with the next generation.

Fozzie Bear is an adviser to the Young Yuksters Club, where comedians-in-training learn the tricks of the trade from masters of the comedic crafts. Fozzie specializes in counterheckling and pelted-fruit avoidance techniques. Gonzo's

Junior Daredevil Scouts are famous for their derring-do and for the universal reluctance of parents to let their children join in this mayhem. And, of course, Animal has long been a role model to the youth of the world, which explains a great deal about why kids act the way they do.

So be a mentor to someone. Share what you know. You may just find that you learn something new yourself.

**FINE ARTS.** Some folks are put off by the term "fine arts." It sounds so highfalutin, conjuring images of stuffed shirts, monocles, and grande dames huffing about the lack of really good caviar this year. Well, I'm here to tell you that the fine arts are for everyone and that the caviar this year is actually pretty good if you know where to shop. Allow me to take you on a guided tour of the fine arts as I've come to know and love them. Ditch the stuffed shirt, toss the monocle, and let's get artsy! Take opera. Many people are put off by the fact that most operas are sung in a language they don't know. This is only because

*Piggy loves the opera because its an excuse to go shopping for a new outfit.*

if they were sung in English, they'd be called musical comedies. Telling folks you're going to a musical comedy doesn't sound nearly as hoity-toity as telling them you're going to the "op-er-ah"! And what's the point of hearing a bunch of people bellow about Sevillian Barbers and Nibelungen Rings if you're not going to sound hoity-toity, right? Ah, but once you actually hear great opera singers, you begin to understand why people swoon at the mere mention of their names. They sing like angels. Their voices fill your soul. And even though you can't understand a word they're singing, you laugh and cry at the pure emotion of it all. Try the opera. And if you can't stand the singing, there is nothing like a great orchestra. Whether you're listening to a full symphony orchestra, a string quartet, or some guy with a concertina and a kazoo, classical music can be a transcendental experience. Bach! Beethoven! Mozart! The beauty of classical music. Or if you'd like something to look at while you listen, consider ballet. As a dancer, I appreciate great dancing. As a frog, I appreciate great leaping. And nothing combines dancing and leaping better than ballet. Whether you're watching a prancing nutcracker or a dying swan, there's something magical about it.

**PROFESSIONAL WRESTLING.** This wasn't my idea, but Gonzo insists that professional wrestling is actually one of the fine arts.

 **It falls somewhere between bog snorkeling and custard diving, but it's definitely one of the big three.**

Rather than debate this point or ask Gonzo what bog snorkeling is, I'll give in. Professional wrestling is a fine art, and watching it can make a fine hobby (if you're into that sort of thing). Gonzo claims that it combines the acrobatics of ballet, the histrionics of opera, and the cacophony of classical music, mixes it with no-holds-barred body-slamming action, and puts it in a steel cage. And you know what? He just might have a point.

**VISUAL ARTS.** Great artwork speaks to us all, especially if you're taking one of those museum audio tours. Great sculptures tell a story. Incredible paintings inspire awe. They capture imagination. And they're great for covering up holes in the wall. Rather than talk about art in the abstract (or talk about abstract art, which I can't make heads or tails of), one hobby many folks enjoy is the study of the visual arts. Whether you're walking around a gallery or curating a collection of your own, surrounding yourself with thought-provoking works is a great way to relax.

**ARTS AND CRAFTS.** After absorbing the fine arts and visual arts, you may be inspired to try your hand (literally) at making something of your own. There are plenty of Muppets whose hobby of choice is handicrafts. Hilda in wardrobe is quite the knitter. Uncle Deadly is learning Bruges lace crochet. Bean Bunny makes miniature dioramas. Even Sam Eagle has attempted needlepoint, considering it to be the most patriotic of crafts. For me, anything having to do with needle precision isn't my strongest suit. But for many, arts and crafts are a terrific way to express yourself and to unwind.

## It's Not That Easy Taking It Easy

So after considering all the hard work that goes into taking it easy, you're probably asking yourself: Why bother?!

The answer is: If you don't make time for yourself, no one else will. Then you'll discover one day that your days have passed and all you've got to show for it is a gold watch, a stack of pay stubs, and some old suits you don't wear anymore. Those are fine things in small doses, but everyone's life needs variety, or in my case, a variety show.

Relaxing may seem like work, but it's well worth the effort. And it really doesn't have to be a major effort. You don't need to buy hundreds of dollars' worth of equipment and be trained by someone wearing goggles and a helmet. Save yourself the time and trouble; chances are that guy in goggles and a helmet is Gonzo, and I know for a fact that he's just making it up as he goes along. Plus, these days, you can learn almost anything on the Internet.

Relaxing should be . . . well, relaxing. It should take you out of your everyday worries and weariness and give you a chance to do something different, get silly, share a meal, ride a roller coaster, or just sit and daydream.

For me, the best way to relax is spending time with family and friends. It lets me enjoy and appreciate life's simple pleasures, like taking a walk, rolling on a log, or dancing in a conga line with chickens. It's my moment to stop and be thankful for all the wonderful, crazy chaos that surrounds me every day.

Take it easy. Embrace the chaos. And if you choose to relax with Gonzo, bring your own parachute.

CHAPTER

15

# Going Green

**T**hese days, everyone seems to be going green. Not in the amphibious sense. (After all, it would be kind of strange if everyone suddenly transformed into a frog. For most folks turning into an amphibian would be awkward.) No, I'm talking about "going green" as in caring about the environment. As a frog who has been green since before he was born, I'm thrilled. But I'm even more excited for my relatives—and for all of the species who happen to be lower on the food chain than humans.

## A Frog's Plan for the Planet

We nonhumans share this planet with you, but you don't often hear directly from us. This may be in large part because most other species don't talk. Oh sure, there's the occasional chatty parrot and almost the entire cast of Muppets,

> **It's a big world with a lot of residents of all shapes, sizes, and colors, so we all have to watch out for one another.**

but for the most part, animals are pretty terse in the presence of humans. Which is how I've become a spokesfrog for all those other species, sharing our thoughts on the best way to keep the planet safe, beautiful, and a happy home for everyone and everything.

Don't worry, I'm not going to scold or get preachy. That's like being told to go clean up your room. Even if you know it needs to be done, no one likes to be told to do it. No, I'm here to encourage you all to keep on doing what you've been doing—making the world cleaner, greener, and a lot less meaner. (Not sure if that's good grammar, but I never could resist a triple rhyme.)

First, I'd like to give you a frog's-eye view of the world. From down here, everything is a lot taller. The trees, the giraffes, Sweetums, you name it—the world is a lot bigger than your average person might imagine.

When you live so close to the ground, you begin to see all the species up close: snakes, lizards, alligators, mosquitoes (yum!), chameleons, turtles, et cetera. And those are just the animals in my particular neck of the swamp. Go to another climate, another ecosystem, and you discover even more animals: lions, tigers, bears (oh my!), cows, horses, pigs, penguins, chickens, and, in the case of Gonzo, whatevers. And as an amphibian, I'm equally familiar with those who dwell underwater—trout, salmon, octopi, whales, jellyfish, and squid, to name just a few. What I'm trying to say is: It's a big world with a lot of residents of all shapes, sizes, and colors, so we all have to watch out for one another.

What can we do? Here are some simple things that each of us can do to make a difference and "go green." And you'll be happy to hear none of these involve turning into a frog.

# 10 Ideas for Keeping It Green

## 1.

### Recycle.

These days, almost everything can be recycled—paper, plastic, glass, etc. You can even "recycle" food by composting. And goodness knows that Fozzie Bear has pioneered the art of recycling jokes. In nature, we recycle naturally. That's where the food chain comes from. Animals (literally) are what we eat. Of course, I'm not suggesting this is a good idea for everyone. For instance, I like the fact that frogs eat mosquitoes, but to be honest I'm not too crazy about the whole herons eating frogs part of the deal. Still, that's the circle of life. So recycle where it makes sense, but don't do it if it means getting eaten by hungry herons.

# 2.
## Eat Greener.

And by this, I don't mean devour frogs. I just mean that taking time to consider where your food comes from and how it was made is one step toward a healthier planet. Whether you grow it yourself, visit a local farmers' market, or look for all-natural products, learning about your food usually leads to tastier meals that are better for the planet. (I don't know about you, but I can really taste the difference in an organic, free-range cricket!) And while you're at it, consider eating greener by ditching the single-use plastic utensils and opting for something reusable or compostable. You'd be amazed at the stories sea turtles tell about all the single-use plastic that ends up in oceans. Basically, consider utensils that either break down naturally, like bamboo, or that you can take home and wash to use again, like metal. The sea turtles will thank you! (Literally. They write incredible thank-you notes, but their letters always arrive drenched.)

# 3.
## Save Energy.

There are so many great ways to save energy these days, from electric vehicles to all kinds of new-fangled lighting and heating and smart appliances. There's a veritable panoply of possibilities, to coin a tongue twister. But there is another, even simpler way to cut down on energy use: Do what Dr. Teeth and the other members of the Electric Mayhem do, which is just "hang out." Nothing saves energy like doing absolutely nothing. Oh, and if you step out of a room, turn off the lights. If you're not watching TV, turn it off. Turning things off can save energy. Our resident experts on this are Statler and Waldorf; those two old guys are well known for turning off the TV the moment Muppets come on the screen—and for turning off the lights the moment we walk into a room. There are friendlier ways to save electricity, but if it works for curmudgeons, it can work for you.

# 4.

## Enjoy Nature.

I know we're talking about the environment, but what better way to protect it than to become an advocate for it? Whether you casually walk in the great outdoors or enjoy more physical activities like hiking, skiing, snowboarding, rock climbing, spelunking, and lots of other wonderful stuff, nature wants you to come visit. (If you're like Gonzo, you can even catapult yourself into a patch of poison ivy, but I don't recommend that.) Staying active and healthy means you can get out there and enjoy the environment more.

# 5.

## Share.

The more we all share, the less we need. For instance, if you have clothes you no longer wear, pass them down to someone else in the family. (This doesn't work for me, but only because frogs spend most of the time naked. On the other hand, Miss Piggy's hand-me-downs could clothe a small country.) And if

you're finished with a joke, give it to Fozzie. He can always use new (used) jokes. Sharing works with lots of stuff we use every day. So share a meal, a grocery bag, a newspaper . . . but I strongly suggest that you don't share your toothbrush.

## 6.

### Shop Secondhand and Mend Old Clothes.

Should you find yourself in the hand-me-down clothing category above, or if you just enjoy scouting the secondhand stores for vintage pocket squares like Uncle Deadly, there is something special about giving clothing a second life. Sure, there's a trend in sustainable fashion so Miss Piggy insists this is au courant, but even beyond the fashionable aspects, it's awfully good for the planet. And it can even feel like a treasure hunt, rummaging through stores and turning other folks' discarded items into treasure! Repair items in need of fixing or mending, restyle or tailor clothing pieces so you can wear them again, and don't discredit the magic of thrift stores. Everyone at The Muppets has their own eclectic style, so I guess we're a little biased when it comes to rewearing old outfits. But it's worked for us all these years, so I'm sure it can work for you, too!

## 7.

### Volunteer.

Whether it's cleaning up a beach or helping at a local animal shelter, working at the recycling center or planting a neighborhood garden, there are plenty of projects in your community that need help. It's not just a great way to do good by the planet; it's also a wonderful chance to meet others who feel the same way you do. If there's one person I admire for his boundless energy and uplifting spirit, it's Walter. You've never met a more enthusiastic volunteer. Even if he doesn't know what he's volunteering for, or is assigned the unglamorous tasks, he rolls up his sleeves and gets to work with a happy whistle in his heart and a spring in his step. I hope we can all be a lot more like Walter.

# 8.
## Keep the World Wet.

Frogs love water. We're born there, so we know how important it is to protect and conserve water. You can: Turn off the tap. Take shorter showers. Fix a dripping faucet. Water the lawn less often. Water is a necessity for everyone, and home for many of us. The more we can do to keep it clean and plentiful, the better for everyone.

# 9.
## Fun in the Sun.

The biggest energy source is right at the center of the solar system. Now, you may not be ready to lead a totally solar-powered life, but you can tap into the hottest name in energy in other ways. For instance, why not dry your

clothes in the sun instead of in a dryer? (This will take longer if you have as many clothes as Miss Piggy, but considerably less time if you walk around naked like me.) And when the weather allows, there's nothing better than getting out of the house and just soaking up some rays yourself. When you do go out in the sun, remember to wear sunblock and stand in the shadow of someone really large—like Sweetums.

# 10.

## Ride a New Way.

You don't have to take a car everywhere. Depending on where you live, you can take a bus, a train, or a subway. As for me, I like to ride a bicycle. This not only cuts down on carbon emissions, it also makes it easier to outrun fast alligators. Of course, I know that this doesn't work for everyone. I mean, for some, riding a bicycle just isn't very convenient. Fish, for instance, have a heck of a time reaching the pedals. But give a thought to better, cleaner ways to get around. Walk, hop, swim . . . however you get there, one thing is for certain: You'll get there greener!

These are just a few ideas. I'm sure you can think of a lot more. Every bit helps. Thanks to folks like you, today it's easier than ever being green. Go ahead, give it a try . . . and give all of us a chance to thrive in this great big wonderful world.

# CHAPTER

## 16

# Creative
# Inspiration

**N**ever get too settled. When you spend too much time resting on your laurels, all you get is a sore backside and a bunch of sorry-looking crushed laurels. You need to seek new challenges, open yourself up to new influences, and find a safe place to put those laurels so they don't get sat on again.

## Staying Current in a Changing World

First, let's talk about staying hip.

This can be a real problem. As you get older, you find yourself longing for "the good old days" when everything was better. The music was livelier, the clothes were snappier, and, most of all, the pains were fewer and farther between.

Now, I'm not that old, so I tried to talk about this phenomenon with our resident elders, Statler and Waldorf, by asking them how they stay hip in an ever-changing world.

**How do we stay hip? Oh, that's easy. Hip replacement surgery.**

**We hardly limp anymore. 'Course, we hardly limp any less. Doh-ho-ho-ho-ho!**

Although Statler and Waldorf may not have been too helpful, they did teach me one thing about staying hip: You should never push it. What exactly do I mean? Well, imagine Sam Eagle with a boho floral romper and micro tattoos. On second thought, don't imagine that.

All I'm trying to say is that you should be only as hip as you want to be. For instance, if there's some new music that just doesn't move you, that's okay.

Listen to the music you like, but keep your ears open to fresh sounds.

Same with fashion; I totally missed the psychedelic '60s style, the polyestered '70s, the big-shouldered '80s, the casual '90s, the naughty aughties, and the layered 2010s. Those styles just weren't me, so I avoided them. And although you may not want to go to the sans-couture extreme that I have, be picky about what you wear; otherwise you'll someday find a box of photos of you wearing a plaid leisure suit and six-inch platforms. And that style hasn't come back around just yet.

Of course, some folks take the exact opposite tack, following every fad foisted on them in the name of pop culture. People like this are sometimes called trendsetters or elite arbiters of taste, but I prefer to call her by name—Miss Piggy. She has never met a fashion trend she hasn't loved or purchased in a variety of sizes and colors.

Whichever path you take to stay hip, remember that although fads quickly fade, you'll be stuck with that tattoo forever. So if you want to stay hip, be open to the whole world, but above all be yourself.

## Sharpening Your Creative Edge

Staying creative is another big challenge. No matter who we are or how daring our creative choices, after a while we all fall into a rut.

At first, Lew Zealand's boomerang fish act was astonishing. But if Lew had kept throwing that same fish year after year, his act would have stunk after a while. He had to keep trying new things, if only just for the halibut.

From the beginning, no one has made more daring creative choices than Gonzo. Yet he'd be just another performance artist/daredevil/whatever were it not for his willingness to seek out new ways to create really loud and colorful explosions while risking life and limb.

Losing that creative edge has happened even to me. I tend to fall back on the same old songs and dance steps. Rather than chase after the unknown, I simply followed along with the familiar. It took real effort to break that cycle of sameness and try something new.

That's how I came up with the following five rules for staying creative. They can help your creative spirit remain original, imaginative, and inspired.

# 1.

## Innovate, Don't Imitate.

Everyone is influenced by others, and that's a good thing. But don't let someone else's style become yours. Take what you learn to another level. Make the dance your own dance. Give the song your own style. Only you can add that one-of-a-kind spark. But, as Gonzo has learned, be careful adding that spark when working with combustibles.

# 2.

## A Spectacular Failure Is Better Than a Humdrum Success.

Go for it! Of course you don't want to fail, but sometimes you will. Don't let fear of failure keep you from trying. And although one can survive on humdrum, same-old, tried-and-true efforts, it's a whole lot more satisfying to reach for the stars, even if you end up landing only on the moon.

# 3.

## Bouncing Ideas.

We all get crazy ideas, but you shouldn't hold them all inside. Share them. In other words, bounce them off one another, off the walls, over the walls, and wherever else they happen to fly. An idea held inside, no matter how crazy it seems, will almost never come to anything. But an idea that literally rebounds around the room is sure to make its mark. Some people call it brainstorming, and if you find yourself in a room with other open-minded people, a lot of fun can be had by bouncing ideas off each other.

## 4.
### Never Forget Whose Shoulders You're Standing On.

As I said, we're all influenced by others. And although I believe that you should never try to copy what's been done before, you should never forget what's been done or who did it. Each of us stands on the shoulders of the generation before us. Appreciate their achievements, 'cause we wouldn't be standing so tall if they weren't here first. This list of pioneers and influences is also helpful when writing awards acceptance speeches.

## 5.
### Make It Up As You Go Along.

Hey, when you're trying to stay creative, too may rules can drive you loopy. Improvise. Let loose! Allow your mind to soar, your heart to leap, and your imagination to do backflips. Because, after all, you can't amaze the world until you first surprise yourself.

Whatever your plans are for staying young at heart and creative, make sure you follow your own instincts. Folks always want you to follow the latest trends, to act in ways that don't feel right. I get edgy whenever someone out here tells me I should "be more edgy." What exactly does that mean?

*Talk about swine-chic. Ooh la la!*

However, I know I can't live in the past and become on old fuddy-duddy. Statler and Waldorf are guaranteed those jobs for life and probably longer. I know that I have to stay current. I have to know who's hot, who's hip, and how to tell the difference. I try to keep up with the times, and so should you. Whether you're in show business or the shoe business, do what works for you. If it doesn't fit, don't force it.

I guess all this comes down to staying curious about the world. Healthy curiosity will help you stay hip and will provide inspiration during those creative ruts. Be curious, ask questions, and never forget to stay young at heart.

CHAPTER

17

# Fridays
## *with*
# Fozzie

**F**ozzie Bear is my best friend. This is not meant as a slight to my other friends. I cherish each of them and feel very lucky to have them in my life. It's just that there's a special bond between Fozzie and me. As I look back, I feel so lucky that I have a best friend at my side on this road trip called life. Which is where this chapter comes in: a reflection on my weekly catch-ups with the fabulous, fuzzy funnyman, Fozzie Bear.

# A Frog, a Bear, and Life's Greatest Lessons

There's not a word yet for old friends who just met, but I felt that inexplicable feeling the first time I met Fozzie. And he's been a huge part of my life ever since then. Maybe it's because we need each other so much.

I know what you're probably thinking: Fozzie is the one who needs me. He's the one who always seems worried. He's the one constantly in need of encouragement. That's one needy bear, all right. And I do my best to meet those needs. I try to take away his worries, give him encouragement, and even punch up his jokes. That's what friends do.

But Fozzie does all that for me and a whole lot more. Y'see, to me, Fozzie is the heart of The Muppets. More than any of us, more than even me. Fozzie believes in the dream. He never, ever gives up on the dream. He always believes. When the hecklers are at their loudest, when the tossed tomatoes are at their ripest, when the mood is dark and the hopes are somewhere between slim and none, Fozzie believes.

I know. I've been there: down in the dumps and up to my eyeballs in trouble. As much as I wish it weren't true, I've wanted to give up, throw in the towel, call it quits, and all that jazz. But Fozzie wouldn't let me.

Nope. When things are at their worst, the bear believes in the dream. But more than that, he believes in me. And that is why Fozzie and I are best friends.

## Making Time for What's Important

Here's how Fridays with Fozzie got started. Although the two of us work together, live in the same house, ride on the same bus, eat at the same table, and sometimes even tell the same jokes, we don't really get to spend much time with each other. I'm usually busy putting together a show, juggling a hundred pressing details with a million big and little problems, mending egos, fending off creditors, and, of course, trying to figure out where the Electric Mayhem parked the bus. And Fozzie is usually busy polishing his act, working day and night to make his jokes funnier, his set tighter, and his exits quicker and safer.

Best friends need time to be with each other, though. Time to talk, laugh, cry, whistle, hum, sing, and just stare out the window and watch the world go by. Our time is Friday.

Every Friday for as long as I can remember, Fozzie and I have made a point of getting together, just the two of us. It's usually late at night, after the final rehearsal, when the theater is quiet and everyone else is out having fun. Our fun is to sit in the front row of the empty theater and be with each other. Some Fridays we'll laugh about the week gone by. And some Fridays we'll swap jokes or try really hard to figure out why there are so many songs about rainbows. But every Friday we talk about life. It's not profound—just two friends sharing time and dreams.

**My favorite way to spend a Friday with Kermit is sitting down and sharing a snack—I like bananas the best 'cause they're so a-peeling! Aah!**

We don't all have a Fozzie in our lives, and that's too bad, because each of us really needs a Fozzie. We all need someone who believes in us and who believes that, no matter how bad things look at the moment, it will work out for the best. We all need someone who carries around a rubber chicken, a buzzer, and a whoopee cushion, just in case. We all need someone who never, ever gives up—on us, on themselves, and on the dream that maybe this time that old joke will get a laugh. Most of all, we all need someone who needs us just as much as we need them.

That's Fozzie.

So go ahead! Get out there! Even if it's not Friday, find your own Fozzie. You'll be very happy you did. A best friend is someone who makes you laugh, even when the jokes aren't funny.

CHAPTER

18

# Life's Like a Movie, Write Your Own Ending

*ou can go through life wondering why you were born a frog, or you can make the most of it. You can wake up each morning just trying to get to the end of the day, or you can do everything in your power to make this your best day ever. You can look around and scratch your head, trying to figure out why you're surrounded by such a strange menagerie of friends and family, or you can be grateful for every moment you get to spend with them. It's up to you.*

## Everyone Is Welcome Here

A lot of people ask me what it is about The Muppets that keeps audiences coming back after all these years. It's a hard question to answer, because I'm just grateful that they do! But if I really think about it, I think there's something special about seeing all different types of personalities and beliefs come together as a group. At The Muppet Theatre, we believe all are welcome and that everyone has something to offer. We've created our own found family where a diva pig can work alongside a patriotic eagle, and where a comedian bear and a banjo-plucking frog can be best friends. We're not here to pass judgment. We're here to tell you you're okay exactly as you are.

As you made your way through this book, examining your own dreams and how you want to reach them, I hope you also learned a little more about what life is like for The Muppets. And maybe you can even take some of our lessons with you on your own journey. Make people feel accepted and welcome. Be comfortable with who you are and what you bring to your stage. Be curious and ask questions. Encourage others. And above all: Don't let life's hecklers stop you from reaching for your dreams.

# Keep Believing, Keep Pretending

I'm not saying it's easy to live each day to the fullest. I'm just saying it's worth trying.

A long time ago, I made a promise to follow my dream. I made that promise to my mom and dad, to my friends, and—most of all—to myself. It's a silly dream, really: singing and dancing and making people happy. But it has kept me going and given me something to believe in every single day.

Fix your heart on a dream and follow it. I can't say where this dream will take you, but I promise it will be the ride of your life. I can't say who you'll meet along the way, but I know they'll be friends that last a lifetime.

That's how I got here. I'm right where I belong, doing just what I set out to do. And best of all, I'm just getting started.

Follow your dream.
I did. And so can you.

**Hi there!**

This is the end of the book. You can put it down now, or share it with a friend. Thanks!